MAKING

F·R·I·E·N·D·S

in the U.K.

The Official Companion
PENNY STALLINGS

CHANNEL 4 BOOKS

Penny Stallings is the author of the bestselling *Previously on Friends: The Official Companion to Seasons 2 and 3* also published by Boxtree as well as *Flesh and Fantasy, Rock 'n' Roll Confidential* and *Forbidden Channels*. She co-created and produced the ABC sitcom *Hi Honey I'm Home* and has provided commentary on art and pop culture for PBS's *The MacNeil-Lehrer NewsHour* and the Bravo Channel since 1984.

First published in 1998 by Boxtree, an imprint of Macmillan Publishers Ltd, 25 Eccleston Place, London SW1W 9NF and Basingstoke

Associated companies throughout the world

ISBN 0 7522 2194 9

Design by Blackjacks

Friends production liaison: Karen Neasi

Photos by Danny Feld, Karen Neasi, Oliver Upton and Laurence Cendrowicz (page 58)
Photo research by Danna Fleishman

1 3 5 7 9 8 6 4 2

A CIP catalogue record for this book is available from the British Library

Printed by Butler and Tanner, Great Britain

Author's special thanks:
Kevin Bright, Marta Kauffman, David Crane, Adam Chase, Michael Curtis, Greg Malins, Seth Kurland, Karen Neasi, Julie Sloane, Adrienne Turner, Francette Levangie, Cacey Riggan, Debra McGuire, Mary Rodriquez, John Shaffner, Julie Heath, Nancy Gould, Jamie O'Connor, Germoney Scott, Phil Gonzales, Shannon Goss, Danny Feld, Danna Fleishman, Victoria Selover, Aimee Chaille, Emma Mann, Emma Tait, Adrian Sington, Barry Secunda, Tim Sarkes, Lee Kernis, Oliver Upton, Greg Grande, Barbara Green, Carol Green and Nicole Parrish

contents

"The One With Ross's Wedding"

In the final episode of the fourth season, we find everyone off to London for Ross's wedding. Everyone, that is, except Phoebe, who can't fly because she's into the last trimester of her pregnancy, and Rachel who feels that it would just be too, you know, "awkward" to watch her ex-boyfriend getting married. That's all. Just awkward.

Once in London, Joey embarrasses Chandler by acting like a typical tourist (which he is) complete with a big, floppy Union Jack hat. Chandler retreats to the relative dignity of his hotel room (but not before embarrassing himself even further by falling into a flower cart). While Chandler sulks, Joey has the best day ever; he even ends up hanging out with Sarah Ferguson who stops to say a few nice words into his video camera about his big, stupid hat.

In the meantime, Ross and Monica have gone with Emily to take a look at Montgomery Hall, the glorious old building Emily has chosen for the wedding ceremony. But as they approach it, they see – to their horror – that it has been partially torn down. Emily is bereft: she's had her heart set on being married here since she was a little girl.

Back home in New York, Phoebe tells Rachel that she's doing really well with the whole Ross-wedding-situation. "If someone I was still in love with was getting married ..." she starts to say, until an indignant Rachel interrupts her. What? She's *not* in love with Ross, she sputters, but her words get all tangled up and she says just the opposite ... that she *is* in love with Ross and she *does* have sexual feelings for him.

Surprisingly, Emily is all smiles when she returns to Ross in their hotel room later that day; you see, she's decided to take Monica's helpful advice and postpone the wedding until they find a proper place. Trying to keep his cool, Ross reminds her that their friends and family have already spent a lot of money to come to London for the wedding. Does she intend to ask them just to write it off? Emily feels that Ross is threatening her with some kind of either/or ultimatum. The wedding is off, she tells Ross tearfully and rushes from the room.

Meanwhile, back in New York, Rachel has decided that Ross deserves to know how she feels (now that she does), so that he can make an "informed decision" about marrying Emily. She's going to London, she tells Phoebe, and that's all there is to it. "It's too late," Phoebe cries, panicking. "You missed your chance. It's over." "It's not over until someone says I do," Rachel tells her as she throws her things into a bag. "I do! I do!" Phoebe calls out frantically, but Rachel is gone.

Back in London, Ross tracks Monica to Joey and Chandler's room and gives her serious grief for meddling in his life. Naturally she's mortified, but she nevertheless manages to bring Ross back around to the real problem: Emily has been dreaming of her wedding since she was a little girl and now those dreams have been dashed in the rubble of Montgomery Hall. Worse still, the man she's picked to marry doesn't seem to understand at all. Okay, now he does, Ross allows, but what's he supposed to do about it? Give Monica the chance to save the day, that's what. (And in a very Monica way at that.) Later that evening, without telling her (or us) why, Monica drags a perplexed Emily back to

Montgomery Hall where Ross is waiting. Inside, Emily discovers that they have given the sad old building a romantic redo, complete with twinkle lights and candles. Emily is touched and thrilled, and the wedding is back on.

Back in New York, Phoebe has begun a determined telephone campaign to stop Rachel from ruining the wedding. She finally gets hold of Joey who promises to "do something". Exactly what that will be, he – and we – have no idea. But Rachel's impromptu visit is the only potential disaster looming on the horizon. At the rehearsal dinner that night, Jack Geller and Emily's father practically come to blows over Jack's share of the so-called wedding expenses – which include, among other things, a gazebo and a wine cellar.

At the next table, Chandler attempts to add a little levity to the proceedings with a Chandler-style toast to the bride and groom, but his jokes bomb badly. Monica, who's not having such a great night herself, attempts to comfort him – until an older, deeply drunk guest mistakes her for Ross's mother. "My mother's right," she wails to Chandler. "I'm never going to get married." Now it's Chandler's turn to do the comforting – which he apparently does quite well since the next time we see them is in bed together the following morning.

The following evening finds the parents still squabbling over money before the ceremony is about to begin. Overhearing the commotion, Emily rushes out from her dressing room. Ross tries to distract her, but is suddenly struck by how beautiful she looks in her wedding gown. Emily cautions him that it's bad

luck for him to see her before the wedding, but he assures her that they've had all the bad luck they're going to have – a perfect cue for Rachel to barge through what's left of the door. Of course, that is just as Rachel pushes past Joey and into the thick of things. Emily exits before noticing her, but Rachel had plenty of time to take in their tender embrace. Suddenly disheartened, she scraps her confession, and instead congratulates Ross and wishes him all the best. She meekly takes a seat among the assembled guests.

As the procession begins, Mrs Waltham's mobile phone rings. It's Phoebe still frantic that Rachel is going to try to ruin the wedding. Joey brings her up to speed as he escorts Mrs Waltham down the aisle. Rachel *did* see Ross, he tells her, but everything's fine – including Felicity, the hot bridesmaid he hooked up with last night. He then holds out the phone so Phoebe can listen to the ceremony.

Next down the aisle are Chandler and Monica. "What we did last night was stupid," Chandler whispers. "What were we thinking?" she hisses back. "I'm coming over tonight though, right?" he then asks quickly. "Oh yeah, definitely," Monica answers, without missing a beat.

At last the ceremony begins, but just as Rachel had done earlier, Ross ends up mangling a crucial declaration. "I, Ross," he repeats after the rector, "take thee, Rachel ..." Realizing what he has said, he quickly corrects himself. "Emily" he shrieks. "*Emily!!!*" As the wedding party and the guests watch in stunned silence, the rector stammers, "Shall I go on?"

London Calling

When Channel 4 first pitched the idea of a *Friends* excursion to London to the show's producers back during the summer hiatus of 1997, the initial reaction was Yeah! Let's do it! But it didn't take long for reality to set in. Marta Kauffman and David Crane already had big things planned for their characters in the coming season. To add a plot turn this complicated, and admittedly, this improbable, was going to require shaking things up in a seismic fashion. And that meant zeroing in on two major unresolved issues that had been hotly debated between them and the writers almost since the show's inception.

"We had two big theoretical decisions to make in these last two shows based on what had been building all season," says writer Michael Borkow. "Did we want Ross to actually get married? And did we want Monica and Chandler to sleep together? There were strong – really strong – feelings both for and against."

The producers put the question to the writing staff: can we accomplish what we've planned for our characters and get them all to England, they asked, and (here's the hard part) make it believable? For two weeks in London – all expenses paid? Does Monica like things clean? Okay, right. But seriously now, they told them, we've got to provide a legitimate reason for the trip that comes out of the characters' personal lives rather than resorting to stale sitcom cliches – like sending them on a glorified sightseeing tour. "We wanted to avoid the usual sort of 'Facts of Life Go to London' thing," says writer Adam Chase. "You know, 'Look … there's Big Ben! Look, there are those guys who don't laugh!'"

An artist's rendering of David and Jeffrey sightseeing in London.

Friends had turned practically every known sitcom convention inside out, why couldn't the same be done here? "A couple of years ago," says writer Michael Curtis, "we had had the same sort of opportunity to take the show to Disneyworld, and it was like, 'Oh, the Friends go to Disneyworld – gross!' But then, when we worked out the stories, we kinda went, 'you know what? We actually have come up with some pretty decent Friends at Disneyworld-type situations.' So when the London thing came up, we went, 'We've been able to think up legitimate, make-sense [group trip] stories in the past, so why couldn't we do the same for London?'"

Okay. But what on earth would make the entire group suddenly feel the need to pick up and prance off to London? Particularly this perpetually poverty-stricken lot – whose idea of big ticket entertainment was ordering in the *two* king-sized pizzas?

"We had to come up with a storyline that would cause all the Friends to go to London," says Greg Malins. "And, so, that ended up being Ross getting married because then they all would *have* to go to his wedding." The only hitch was, how do you get from "Ross-meets-someone" to "Ross-is-going-to-England-to-get-married" in six episodes?

Enter Emily – the lovely young niece of Rachel's boss who happened to be visiting New York from London. Rachel has promised to look after Emily while she's in town, but she ends up foisting her off onto a reluctant Ross. But this turns out to be the nicest thing she's ever done for him. (Except maybe when she did her Princess Leia bit.) It's only a matter of days before Ross finds himself smitten – as is Emily (and as are we). But being rational people

"We wanted to say thank you to all the British Friends fans. And we just wanted to come to London!" Friends co-creator David Crane tells reporters at the Channel 4 press conference.

Director Kevin Bright calls the shots.

Matthew Perry, Marta Kauffman, make-up department head Robin Seigel, Matt Le Blanc and Adam Chase watch the playback of Joey and Chandler's Westminster Abbey contretemps.

Who holds up the people who hold up the show? Kevin Bright's assistant Karen Neasi gives a boost to producer Marta Kauffman.

(well, Emily is anyway), they agree that their liaison will last only the length of her two-week visit. But Ross is heartsick at the idea of her going home. (Even though Emily has considerately left a pair of her knickers under his pillow for him to remember her by.) Come live with me, he suddenly blurts out. But how can she leave London? She has a family, a job, a life. And besides, she tells him, it's not like it's a long time from now and we were thinking of getting married or something. Ross quickly fixes that by proposing on the spot. Emily can't believe him – and she can't believe herself, but she accepts just as impetuously. So what if they've only known each other for two weeks? Emily makes Ross feel like an entirely new man. Hey, he got his ear pierced. He even signed up for helicopter lessons. And he likes that man and wants him to hang around. But there is just one little – actually, big – question: is Ross really capable of wiping Rachel out of his psyche just like that? Maybe. Maybe not.

The more the plotline was tweaked, the more complicated it became – particularly from a production standpoint. And then NBC, the show's American parent network, got into the act with a proposal that the London episode be expanded from one to two shows which would then be shown as an hour-long special. All of a sudden, a standard location shoot was turning into the equivalent of a feature-length film. The word ambitious didn't begin to cover the ordeal the whole undertaking was shaping up to be. But the truth is that both the cast and crew have a soft spot for their British fans. So it was gonna be tough. So what? "The London trip was our valentine to our British fans," David Crane explained at the show's press conference. "London called us. And we called it right back."

Friends co-creator David Crane, assistant director Ben Weiss and writer Michael Borkow confer with the cast during a break in filming back home in Los Angeles.

They just wanna make you laugh: clockwise from top left – writers Shana Goldberg-Meehan, Scott Silveri, Andrew Reich, Amy Toomin, Jil Condon, Seth Kurland, assistant Mark Kunerth, Greg Malins, Wil Calhoun, assistant Richard Goldman, Adam Chase, David Crane, Michael Curtis, Marta Kauffman, Michael Borkow, Kevin Bright and assistant Alicia Sky Varinataitis.

A Brief History Of The Friends And Their Lovers

When *Friends* first announced that it was coming to London to shoot its final show of the season, it was widely rumoured that the episode's storyline would involve the marriage of one of the characters. Given the events of the prior three years, the most likely candidates appeared to be Ross and Rachel. But why would they get married in England? And if not Ross and Rachel, then who?

One thing was certain: a marriage scenario wasn't likely to include Chandler or Joey – committed non-committees that they are. And Phoebe hadn't exactly been spending her time hunting down marriage material, which is probably all to the good since her taste in men – like her taste in everything else – leans toward the bizarre. Like, for example, she once had a thing for a guy who was stalking her. And she was seriously smitten with a guy whose private parts had a tendency to fall out of his pants. But be that as it may, Phoebe was otherwise engaged – what with her uterus incubating her brother's triplets. (She does have a special moment with a miniature pug dog this season, but that's only because it's possessed by the spirit of her dead mother.)

When you look back, you realize that each of the Friends has had a serious run-in with The Thing Called Love. Even Joey. (Yes, Joey.) It wasn't so very long ago that the perennial heartbreaker had his own heart broken by the beautiful Kate – an actress, who, while she liked him a lot, was far more in love with getting her name in lights than she ever could be with any guy.

What if Monica and Chandler did become romantically involved? Would it be the end of a beautiful friendship?

Joey and Chandler get into the spirit of things as Rachel throws an impromptu (and unwelcome) going-away party for Emily.

And speaking of Chandler (actually, we weren't: but let's do), when it comes to the Unlucky-at-Love Sweepstakes, there is no more battle-scarred contender than the loveable Chandler Bing. His most serious romantic involvement to date has been with ("oh-my-God") Janice, who liked him too – but apparently not as much as she liked her ex-husband. But Chandler seems finally to have gotten Janice out of his system. In fact, he'll go – literally – to Yemen rather than expose his sensitive soul to her leopard skin-covered wiles again.

This year, as in years past, Chandler will find other lost causes to make his life miserable. There is Kathy, another actress and an all-round great girl who happens to be going with Joey. (Don't you hate it when that happens?) Chandler is so attracted to her that he'll risk losing his best friend to win her. And that's what ends up hurting Joey most about the whole deal. Girls come and go. Or anyway, they do with Joey – but best friends, best *guy* friends … that's forever. Or anyway, it should be. The two eventually manage to work things out (after Chandler spends some contemplative time in the entertainment unit). And that's a good thing since Kathy hasn't been with Chandler more than a few weeks before she falls in

love with her co-star in an off-off-(off) Broadway play. (You can't really blame her; they were both naked for most of the show.)

For Chandler, as for Joey, girls come and girls go, but there is one who's always there to torment him – and she lives right across the hall. Not that Chandler has ever actually allowed himself to admit just how much he is attracted to Monica. And not that he would ever want her to know how he feels – that is, unless there were a chance she might feel something too. But instead of laying it on the line, Chandler invents all sorts of what-if scenarios (like, "So what if you and I were together?") that end up making Monica laugh (a lot) – which, in turn, leaves Chandler (deeply) depressed. By the end of the third season, the closest Chandler had come to intimate contact with Monica was when he peed on her leg after she was stung by a jellyfish at the beach.

And Monica? As far as she was – and is – concerned, she is the ultimate loser at love. Of course, there was that celebrated period during the show's

It might not look like it, but Chandler seems finally to have gotten Janice out of his system this season.

second and third seasons when it looked as though she might actually marry Dr Richard Burke. It was clear that they had the perfect relationship. Sure, he was a little (okay, a lot) older. Old enough, in fact, to be a close pal of her parents. But hey, the man looked like Tom Selleck. In fact, the man *was* Tom Selleck. And that counted for a lot. Still, Monica wanted to start a family – so much so that at one time she had even contemplated making a withdrawal from a sperm bank. But how could she ask Richard – a man with grown children – to start a family again? He reluctantly offered to start all over with Monica, if that's what it would take to have her, but she could see that was a recipe for disaster. That's the thing about Monica … she's very practical. (Sometimes *too* practical.) And that's the thing about *Friends*: even with the monkey and the palatial New York digs, it manages to stay believable. And asking us to swallow the idea that Monica would give up her dream of children – or that she would ask Richard to go through raising a family all over again – would strain credulity even more than seeing a chick and a duck existing

Tom Selleck (the real guy) says that he was overcome with jealousy the first time he tuned in to see Monica dating after their big break-up.

happily in a New York apartment. So, with Richard out of the picture, just who would Monica be marrying? The rich guy, Pete Becker? Sure she liked him, but that was just it; she *liked* him. He was no Tom Selleck. (Although he *was* hot young actor Jon "Swingers" Favreau.) She tried. She really did – with Julio, the poet/busboy and even Jean Claude Van Damme and this year with a guy she'd known back in high school, but try as she may, she couldn't kick her thing for Richard. Maybe that's what made her consider getting involved with Richard's son – a handsome young doctor. But the ramifications of that were just too icky. So, for now, if she can't be a bride, she'll content herself with playing bride by secretly dressing up in Emily's wedding gown.

Which brings us back to Ross and Rachel.

Were They Really on a Break?

We came back from the summer to find Ross and Rachel in a brief cessation of hostilities, but that respite was short-circuited when he refused (again) to admit to cheating with Chloe, the girl from the Xerox place. But even though Rachel was (technically) correct in her charge, what she didn't know – and we did – was how defenceless Ross had been on the night of his little indiscretion. Could his blunder really be classified as cheating? And if so, was he completely to blame? After all, Rachel had just hit him with "The Break" ultimatum and he was completely desolate. So he went to a bar and got drunk. So then he was drunk *and* desolate. And anyway, the Xerox Girl was deeply sexy. "I thought we were over," Ross told Rachel as he begged her forgiveness. But she was unmoved. He was a totally different person to her now, she told him, and what they'd had together was changed forever.

A few weeks later, Rachel gave Ross back all that remained of their time together – a box of his old junk. He had no choice but to accept the cold, hard truth: he and Rachel were over. Reluctantly, he

moves on to a new girl, a perky blond named Bonnie. But then, Ross is that kind of guy. Unlike the Joeys of the world, Ross is not afraid to admit that he's looking for a relationship. He laid it right on the line from the very first show: "I don't *want* to be single," he whined. "I just want to be married again." And, in fact, he was the only one in the group to have taken the plunge (unless you count Phoebe's faux marriage to a gay – she thought – Canadian ice dancer). And he had only known Julie (the palaeontologist) a few weeks before they were thinking of getting a cat. (Translation: moving in together.) And now here he was, just a few months after the big Break, starting to get serious about Bonnie.

While Ross sought the comfort of a monogamous relationship, Rachel expended most of her time and energy on work. She had a few dates with Mark, the assistant buyer who helped her get her job, and this season she even tries to get something going with a (much) younger man and, more seriously, with Joshua, a dishy lawyer she met at work. For a while there, Rachel thought Joshua might actually be The Guy. In fact, she even asked him to marry her after only four

The minute Rachel and Ross were on a 'break' Mark moved in on Rachel. (It turns out Ross was right about him all along.)

Ross was crazy about Bonnie until Rachel talked her into shaving her head.

dates. Okay, maybe it was a little premature, but Rachel was feeling somewhat pressured; after all, Ross was getting married (not that she cared) and besides, he had the nerve to ask her "how she was" with it. (The nerve!) Not only was she all right, she heatedly assured him, it just so happened that she and Joshua were A Thing. But not only were she and Joshua not A Thing; they weren't even a thing. The poor guy ran for the hills after she opened the door wearing a wedding gown. (She was playing dress-up with Monica and Phoebe.) In truth, most of Rachel's attempts to get something going with other guys has usually ended up in a stew – primarily because through all these entanglements, always hovering somewhere in the background, was the spectre of Ross. Ross the Infuriating. Ross the Real Thing.

Sometimes Rachel has a hard time telling Ross how she really feels, but this wasn't one of those times.

Rachel does a good job of hiding her feelings about Ross's wedding plans – even from herself. She insists she's happy for him, but there's no way she can bring herself to actually go to the wedding. "It's just gonna be too hard," she tells the others. "It's Ross. How can I watch him get married?"

But even if Ross did something totally crazy – like say Rachel's name instead of Emily's during his wedding vows – would Rachel ever be able to bring herself to commit to him once and for all? Or anyone else – for that matter? As the very first episode of *Friends* made hilariously obvious, Rachel has a marked ambivalence towards the institution of marriage. The first look we got at her was as a runaway bride who had somehow ended up in a West Village coffee house. She had given up certain security as a Long Island dentist's wife – for what? She certainly didn't know. Shopping was her only real talent and that didn't qualify her for much. In order to keep herself afloat she had no choice but to take a job right then and there – in the place she'd landed – Central Perk. And so she did – surprising both herself and her old friend, Monica. And while she may not have been the best waitress in the world (in fact, she may have been the worst), she was, at last, becoming her own person. So much so that even as she and Ross became more serious about each other, she let him know in no uncertain terms that she had no intention of getting stuck in the suburbs raising children. He was shocked, but we weren't. We could see how she was changing and growing. She was not that spoiled little rich girl Ross had pined after in high school. She wasn't even a waitress any more. After flailing around at various jobs, she'd finally managed to land the vaunted position of assistant lingerie buyer at Bloomingdales. (Maybe shopping *did* qualify her for something after all.) Okay, it wasn't brain surgery, but it was a for-real triumph for her.

Maybe Ross and Rachel were on a break. Maybe they weren't. Either way, Chloe, the girl from the Xerox place, was REALLY sexy.

She'd gone from pampered princess to waitress to a place where she could dress – and even act – like a grown-up. No longer a child-woman dependent on others for her survival, Rachel Green had a good job, great friends and, best of all, a discount at Bloomingdales. No doubt about it, life was sweet.

Ross had been proud of her too – up to a point. Even so, he had never been able to allow Rachel her space. Maybe it was all those years of watching other men – who loved her less – treat her indifferently (or worse). Whatever it was, try as he might, he couldn't control his jealousy. And that created all sorts of emotional smash-ups – like the time he barged into Rachel's office thinking she was making out with Mark, only to discover Mark making out with his own girlfriend. Even after that humiliation, he couldn't shake the picture of Rachel with Mark he carried around in his mind. Particularly as Rachel began staying late at the office more often. What could she be doing till all hours of the night? Before long, Ross

was acting like a less enlightened man than we knew him to be. It was a lethal combination of concern and distrust that prompted him to surprise her with a picnic supper at her office on a night when she had to work late. He was worried about her, he told her, he wanted to help. He meant well, sort of, but none of that mattered after he accidentally set her papers on fire while trying to arrange a candle-lit dinner on her desk. Rachel had repeatedly warned him that he was suffocating her – and this time, he almost did.

The fire set spinning a series of events that ultimately led to their infamous Break. And that's where we left them at the end of the third season. Not together. And not apart. By the beginning of the fourth year, Ross had once again taken on the role of Rachel's punching bag – which is how he ends up with the woman of his dreams. And that's where you'll find him as you finish reading this page. With Emily. Tart, smart and totally not Rachel. And that's fine by him. Miracle of miracles, Ross is happy at last. (Isn't he?)

The One You Were Never Supposed To See

You know that the actors on *Friends* don't just walk in front of the cameras and start spouting all those funny lines off the top of their heads. (Well, don't you?) But what you might not realize is that every aspect of what you see has been fastidiously faceted and polished – for hours, for days, for weeks at a time – by those people whose names whizz by at the beginning and end of the show. No doubt about it: it takes a serious expenditure of brain cells to mould a script's early motifs into the mean machine that will ultimately glide into your living room.

So, the way we figure it is: if we're going to deconstruct every bit of history surrounding the making of *Friends* in the UK for your entertainment and edification, we might as well go all the way and let you have a look at the very earliest version of the script, which we'll call, "The One You Were Never Supposed to See". This draft (called the first or "table" draft in sitcom parlance, because the actors read it aloud for the first time while sitting around a banquet-sized table) presents the story of Ross's wedding as it was originally plotted, complete with the writers' notes to themselves and each other indicating ways to tweak, rearrange and revamp it.

In the first version, the gang was headed to London for the last two episodes of the show. But by the time the script was finalized many weeks later, six new guest stars had been added and the two shows had been merged into a one-hour special. These welcome – but nerve-racking – developments required that David Crane hole up in a room in the London Marriott Hotel with the writers for the better part of the stay. "Shooting Ross's Wedding was like doing two production weeks crammed into one – with jet-lag …" says Adam Chase. "We just moved the writers' room to London for a couple of weeks." The staff split into two groups that rotated shifts but still ended up with everyone working late into the night. Meanwhile, out on location, director Kevin Bright put the story into motion and Marta Kauffman edited and fed new lines to the actors. With each change, the story's tension built in a more dramatic manner and, best of all, the characters became more themselves. While it's true that this draft of Ross's Wedding gives you a look at *Friends* with its knickers down, we think you'll find it every bit as funny as the one that makes it to air. And as you follow the televised show along with the final script, you'll see yet another version – this one revised even further by way of the cast's ingenious comic performances as well as the writers' last-minute additions.

Now it's your turn to see how *Friends* works from the inside out. Have fun!

Some Key Changes to Look For in the First or "Table" Draft:

➔ David Crane's note to PUMP UP the excitement in the opening "teaser" causes the action to go from some light-hearted talk about London to an imminent departure and a crazed Monica, sure that everyone is going to miss their flight and ruin their lives forever.

➔ Rachel reveals right from the opening sequence that she is upset over the wedding – whereas in the final version, the fact that she is still in love with Ross will dawn on her much later, thanks to a helpful hint from Phoebe.

➔ The gang doesn't travel to London together. Look for the long riff with the wedding presents to delay Joey and Chandler's arrival to London by a day.

➔ One interim draft of the script had Chandler ordering Joey to "stop reading my condoms" as Joey tries to figure out the Spanish writing, but ultimately the joke was pulled entirely. Condom jokes are never a favourite of the network censors, but in this case, the joke was scrapped for another, more important, reason: one of the writers didn't get it.

➔ Phoebe's Ross and Emily PUPPETS are a riot but while such bits of funny business often make their way into subsequent scripts, writer Michael Borkow says that this probably won't because "It's just too tied to the wedding." (Too bad.)

➔ Much of Chandler and Joey's bickering – along with a trip to a London McDonald's – will be condensed into an hilarious spat over a walk-in map.

...And in the Final Draft:

➔ At the end of Act I, the crisis goes from losing the wedding hall to an ugly fight that causes Emily to call off the wedding altogether. This causes Ross to have an accident with his pants zipper that will anticipate a soon-to-be infamous sequence in the movie hit, THERE'S SOMETHING ABOUT MARY.

➔ Jack Geller's confusion over the "tube" – which embarrasses Monica and Ross as the Gellers meet Emily's parents – will be moved further down in the action so as to crank up Monica's motivation to get depressed and drunk, and later into bed with her good friend, Chandler Bing.

➔ In the first draft, Ross doesn't know that Monica's meddling was to blame for Emily's decision to postpone the wedding; in the final script, Ross knows, but Monica doesn't. And while Chandler and Joey hide in the bathroom during both confrontations, they don't get paranoid about the way it might, you know, look until the final version.

➔ In the final draft, Emily's parents are transformed from an innocuous couple to the in-laws of Ross's nightmares. Mrs Waltham – now Emily's step-mother – is one of those frighteningly haughty females who can silence her husband with a single (blood-curdling) look. And Steven Waltham, although a pussycat by comparison, almost comes to blows with Jack Geller over his share of the wedding expenses.

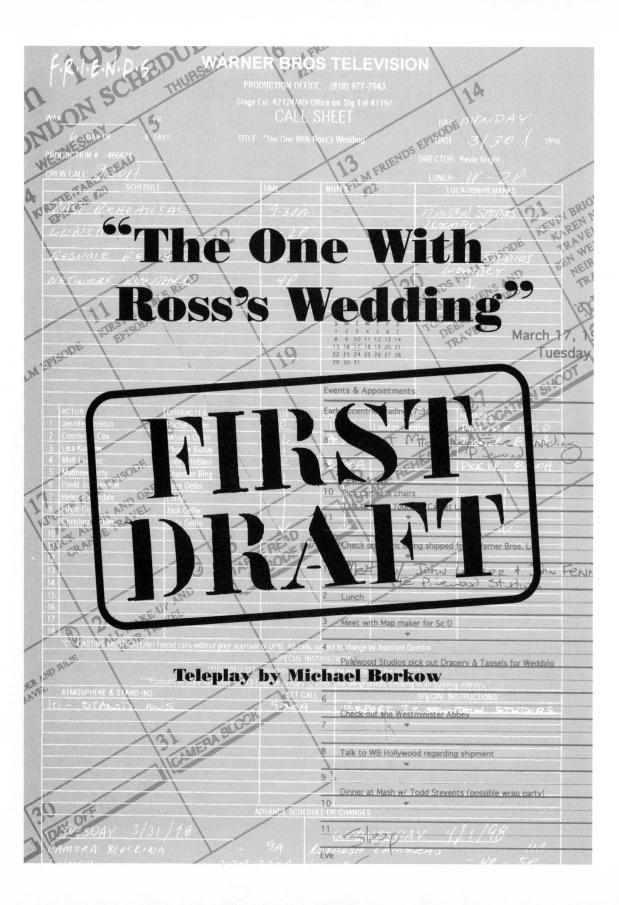

"The One With Ross's Wedding"

FIRST DRAFT

March 17, 19__
Tuesday

Teleplay by Michael Borkow

<u>"The One With Ross's Wedding"</u> FIRST DRAFT

<u>TEASER</u>
<u>SCENE A</u>

FADE IN: <u>INT. COFFEE HOUSE - DAY</u> (THE GROUP, MINUS
JOEY AND ROSS, IS HANGING OUT. <u>JOEY ENTERS</u>, WITH A
BUNCH OF TOUR BOOKS AND MAPS.

                    JOEY
    All right, I got London all figured out.

                    MONICA
    Look at you with all the books.

                    JOEY
    Well, I'm getting excited. I've never been
    out of the country before. Except once. I
    was in Canada for a few minutes. I was lost.

                    CHANDLER
    But now you know. When you leave Manhattan,
    it's a left, not a right, if you're heading
    to Fort Lauderdale.

JOEY NODS.

                    MONICA
    (OFF GUIDE BOOK) Ooh, Buckingham Palace.

                    PHOEBE
    You guys have to bring back pictures.

                    MONICA
    (REALIZING) Oh, god, here we are going on
    about London, and you can't even go. I'm
    sorry.

                    JOEY
    (TO PHOEBE) Yeah, sorry.

                    MONICA
    (NOTICES PICTURE) Ooh, Westminster Abbey!

                    JOEY
    Yeah, we're going to the Abbey.

                    JOEY/MONICA
    (TO PHOEBE) Sorry. Yeah, sorry.

[handwritten right margin] WHAT IF WE START THE SHOW WITH THEM LEAVING FOR THE PLANE? MORE ENERGY! MORE EXCITEMENT!! MORE SENSE OF EVENT! —D.C.

[handwritten] you got it

[handwritten] How about some Monica Mania?

<u>"The One With Ross's Wedding"</u> FIRST DRAFT

>   PHOEBE
> If you're so sorry, maybe you shouldn't go.
> Stay here. We can hang out. (OFF THEIR
> LOOKS) I thought so.

<u>RACHEL ENTERS</u>. AD-LIB HELLOS.

>   MONICA
> (TO RACHEL) So, by any chance, have you
> changed your mind about going to Ross's
> wedding?

>   RACHEL
> No. I just know it'd be too hard.

>   THE OTHERS
> Yeah. That sucks. We'll miss you.

>   PHOEBE
> But ask them to stay and see what
> happens.

>   CHANDLER
> I'm sure Ross understands.

>   RACHEL
> No, he doesn't. He doesn't <u>know</u> why I can't
> go, and I really don't want to get into that
> with him.

>   PHOEBE
> What reason did you give him?

>   RACHEL
> I told him I was too busy at work.

>   PHOEBE
> Oh, so you already have a reason. I was
> gonna say, he was totally understanding when
> I told him I was having three babies.
>   FADE OUT:

[Handwritten margin notes: "TOO EARLY? REVEALS RACHEL'S AMBIVILENCE" with arrow and "yes, lets lose." bracketing the RACHEL through CHANDLER section; "on RACHEL'S FACE WE" pointing to the final lines]

"The One With Ross's Wedding" FIRST DRAFT

ACT ONE

SCENE ONE

FADE IN: <u>INT. MONICA & RACHEL'S APT. - THAT NIGHT</u> (NIGHT 1) PHOEBE'S LYING ON THE COUCH. RACHEL'S HANGING OUT. MONICA'S BAGS ARE PACKED, AND SHE'S GOING THROUGH HER CARRY-ON. <u>SFX: KNOCK ON DOOR</u>. MONICA OPENS THE DOOR. <u>ROSS ENTERS</u>. AD-LIB HELLOS.

> ROSS
> I got a cab waiting. You all set?

> MONICA
> Yep. You have the tickets?

> ROSS
> (SHOWS THEM) Got 'em right here.

> PHOEBE
> I'd come over there and hug you, but it's too hard for me to get up.

> ROSS
> (STARTS TOWARDS PHOEBE) Oh, then I'll come hug —

> PHOEBE
> Bring me that newspaper. Since you happen to be coming over here.

HE TURNS BACK, TAKES THE NEWSPAPER OFF THE KITCHEN TABLE, AND BRINGS IT TO PHOEBE. AS THEY HUG...

Smart girl: Phoebe takes full advantage of everyone's guilt about abandoning her to go to London by getting them to wait on her hand and foot.

<u>"The One With Ross's Wedding" FIRST DRAFT</u>

                    PHOEBE (CON'T.)
        And Mon, I want to hug you, too.

MONICA, WHO'S ABOUT TWO STEPS AWAY, STARTS FOR PHOEBE

                    PHOEBE (CON'T.)
        And you might as well bring me my book. It's
        on the counter in the guy's apartment.

                    MONICA
        (NOT PLEASED) You got it.   *(let's give this*
                                             to Chandler

<u>SHE EXITS</u>.

                    ROSS
        (TO RACHEL) So...

                    RACHEL
        (HUGS HIM) Have fun.

                    ROSS
        Come.

                    RACHEL
        What?

                    ROSS
        Come. The guys aren't leaving till
        tomorrow. You could fly with them.   *Super*
                                                  Casual
<u>MONICA ENTERS</u>, WITH PHOEBE'S BOOK.

                    PHOEBE
        Thank you so much.

MONICA STANDS BY WAITING FOR HER HUG.

                    PHOEBE (CON'T.)
        (NOTICING) Oh, right.

PHOEBE GIVES HER A CURSORY HUG AND OPENS UP HER BOOK.

"The One With Ross's Wedding" FIRST DRAFT

She wants
him back ...

But only if he'll
admit they were
NOT on a break.

"The One With Ross's Wedding" FIRST DRAFT

He won't ...

But he still wants her to come to the wedding. After all, they're still friends. Aren't they?

<u>*"The One With Ross's Wedding"* FIRST DRAFT</u>

                    RACHEL
Ross. I told you. I have work.

                    ROSS
I mean I could understand if this was about
us...

                    RACHEL
Excuse me, "Mr. Center of the Universe."
Not everything is about you. This actually
happens to be about the fact that I have
a very important job. If I'm not there to
help them, there's a lot of rich old
people who will be walking around
Manhattan with clothes that don't match.

Love this, but it's going to blow Rachel's turnaround later!!! Cat?

                    ROSS
Well, that does sound a lot more important
than going to a friend's wedding. (THEN, TO
MONICA) Let's go

too emotional

HE GRABS MONICA'S BAGS. THEY ALL AD-LIB GOODBYES, AND
<u>ROSS AND MONICA EXIT</u>. RACHEL WATCHES THEM GO, SAD.
PHOEBE REACHES FOR HER DRINK ON THE COFFEE TABLE, BUT
SHE CAN'T QUITE REACH IT. SHE LOOKS AT RACHEL.
DISSOLVE TO:

                    <u>SCENE C</u>

<u>INT. CHANDLER & JOEY'S APT. - THE NEXT DAY</u> (DAY 2)
(Chandler, Joey, Phoebe, Rachel) JOEY SEES CHANDLER
PUT SOMETHING IN HIS LUGGAGE.

                    JOEY
What's that?

                    CHANDLER
Condoms, baby. I didn't hook up
at the last wedding we went to,
but I'm not getting discouraged,
since that was a lesbian wedding.

> 66 To do Joey, I have to
> turn half my brain off.
> The problem is, at
> the end of the day,
> I sometimes forget to
> switch it back on again. 99
> MATT LE BLANC

"The One With Ross's Wedding" FIRST DRAFT

How about "don't read my condom"

JOEY
(LOOKS AT BOX) Why's the writing in Spanish?

Does this make sense? I don't get it, but then again I didn't go to college... —GM

CHANDLER
(EMBARRASSED) I did a semester abroad.

> "I'm really similar to Chandler in that I'm most comfortable in a world that's kind of funny. If there's an awkward pause at all in a conversation, I'll fill it as fast as I can with a joke."
> MATTHEW PERRY

PHOEBE AND RACHEL ENTER. AD-LIB HELLOS.

RACHEL
We just came over to wish you guys a good trip.

JOEY
Oh, that's nice. (MOVES A BAG OFF CHAIR) Here, Phoebe, have a seat.

Find out what those British chocolate biscuit thingies are. M.

<u>"The One With Ross's Wedding"</u> FIRST DRAFT

                    PHOEBE
        Don't think so. Next place I sit, I sit for
        a month.

CHANDLER STUFFS A BIG PORCELAIN BOWL INTO A BAG.

                    CHANDLER
        I can't believe Monica convinced me to bring
        her wedding gift for her.

                    RACHEL
        (SHOCKED) What? We're not all getting
        them something together?

                    PHOEBE
        No. I'm making them puppets.

SHE PULLS OUT TWO IDENTICAL PIECES OF PLAIN COTTON.

                    PHOEBE (CON'T.)
        This is Ross. And this is Emily.

                    RACHEL
        (TO CHANDLER AND JOEY) You guys want to go
        in on something?

                    CHANDLER
        Sorry. We got them an electric race track.

                    PHOEBE
        That's not very romantic.

                    JOEY
        Yeah, it is. The cars glow in the dark.

                    PHOEBE
        (IMPRESSED) Ooooh.

                    RACHEL
        That is terrible. What am I gonna get them?
        It can't be too meaningful, because he'll
        know I care too much.

Handwritten annotations:

DO WE NEED ALL THIS? IT'S FUN, BUT WE WANT TO GET TO LONDON, BABY! —D.C.

If we show a race track. Maybe the company will send us a free one for the office. MB

← I think BRIAN DOYLE ACTUALLY DID This! G.M.

too soon!

It Was All Very Cloak And Dagger

*a*s soon as word leaked out that *Friends* was coming to England to shoot the top-secret final episode of the fourth season, press coverage of the event exploded with a flurry of rumours and speculation. There was to be a wedding – that much the show's producers had confirmed. But who? And why London?

Nailbiter for Friends

JUST GOOD FRIENDS?

Matthew Perry signs autographs for the fans during a break in filming.

FRIENDS heart-throb Ross may marry his English sweetheart after all.

EXCLUSIVE
BY SHARON MARSHALL

But after the audience left, an alternative ending was shot to

all very cloak and we knew word wo and we want to fans guessing

SHE is about to become so much more than Friends.

Helen Baxendale has joined the cast of the hit

Banner-sized headlines trumpeted the marriage rumours weeks before the show arrived – with Monica (Monica?) and Ross favoured as the most likely candidates for what inevitably would be matrimonial mayhem. With this, the press seemed to know something that even the show's creators didn't, since, in reality, they were still back home in Los Angeles grappling with how the story would unfold.

By the time the cast members departed for London, photographers were already on hand to record their departure from the Los Angeles Airport – where one happened to catch Jennifer Aniston falling as she exited an escalator. Big, splashy tabloid photos of the non-event greeted her when she arrived at Heathrow the next day. Throughout their stay, the actors were trailed by photographers and reporters who followed them around to their hotels, out to restaurants and on shopping excursions. In breathless prose, articles proclaimed the guys hunky and the girls gorgeous or dishevelled or both. But be it snippy or adoring, the non-stop coverage made it plain *Friends* was *The* Big News in London.

"The One With Ross's Wedding" FIRST DRAFT

                        CHANDLER
        Hmm. What kind of message do you think our
        gift says?

                        PHOEBE
        That you guys want something to play with
        when you go to their house.

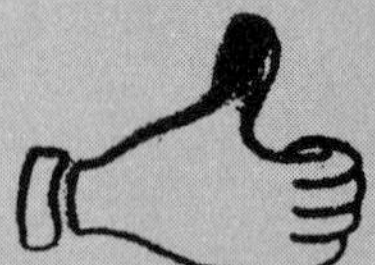

                        JOEY
        (TO CHANDLER) Great, so we don't have to put
        it on the card.

                        CHANDLER
        Well, we should go.

                        JOEY
        London, baby!
        THEY PICK UP THEIR BAGS AND HEAD FOR THE DOOR.

ESTABLISHING EXTERIOR SHOTS

                        DISSOLVE TO:

                        SCENE D

        INT. ROSS'S HOTEL SUITE – THE NEXT DAY
        (DAY 3) ROSS IS WITH ALL THE PARENTS.
        MONICA COMES OVER.

                        MONICA
        So, you're planning to serve chicken,
        huh? Salmon's much more sophisticated.

                        ROSS
        The food is set, Monica. We're having
        chicken.

        EMILY PASSES BY, ON THE PHONE.

                        EMILY
        (INTO PHONE) No, no, no, you're not
        getting it. The wedding is this Sunday.
        (TO THE OTHERS) This florist is driving
        me mad.

        SHE CROSSES AWAY. MONICA CROSSES TO EMILY.
        ROSS TURNS TO THE PARENTS.

                        ROSS
        (OFF CHART) What if we sit Aunt Susan at
        this table, and Aunt Joan at this table?

Handwritten notes:

MATT IS GREAT WITH THIS. LET'S PUMP IT UP!

Karen. Call Wendy KNOLLER & get her to find out if we could get "LONDON Calling" by the Clash to use here K.B.

We should probably change the names. My Aunt Susan & Aunt Joan don't usually watch the show, but just in case... MB

<u>"The One With Ross's Wedding"</u> FIRST DRAFT

> JACK GELLER
> If a piece of cake can fly that far, you
> don't want to risk it.

do we need?

> STEVEN WALTHAM
> Look, if there's a chance of these two
> actually getting in a fight and some
> bystander getting hurt...(TO HIS WIFE) why
> don't we sit them next to your brother?
> (UNDER HIS BREATH) Bloody junkie.

MEANWHILE, EMILY'S ON THE PHONE, WITH MONICA
LISTENING.

> EMILY
> (INTO PHONE) Yes, orchids, roses and
> marigolds... You can't do marigolds
> by Sunday?

WHAT ARE MARIGOLDS DOING IN HERE?!
YOU CAN TELL A GUY WROTE THIS

> MONICA
> (LEANS IN) Tulips?

> EMILY
> (INTO PHONE) Tulips?...Oh, splendid.

MONICA CROSSES TO ROSS.

> MONICA
> (PROUD) The tulips were my idea.

Whats wrong with marigolds? Signed. A Guy

> ANDREA WALTHAM
> Well, we have to pick up some guests
> at the airport. We'll see you all tonight.

> JUDY GELLER
> Why don't we go as well? I'd love
> to ride the Tube.

Are we okay on this joke?
YEAH, THE CENSOR'S NOT COMING TO LONDON.

> JACK GELLER
> (SHOCKED) Judy! We just met these
> people.

Right?
— G.M.

> JUDY GELLER
> The Tube is what they call their subway,
> dear.

> JACK GELLER
> Oh.

<u>"The One With Ross's Wedding"</u> FIRST DRAFT

<u>THE</u> <u>PARENTS</u> AD-LIB GOODBYES AND <u>EXIT</u>.

                    EMILY
(HANGS UP) Aargh! (TO MONICA) All right,
we have an hour to pick up your brides-maid
dress, and on the way we can show you
the hall.

                    MONICA
Oh, great.

                    EMILY
(TO ROSS) And the flowers will be there
Sunday at four.

                    ROSS
But the caterer needed them there at three.
(OFF HER LOOK) You know that. Should we call
the caterer? (OFF HER LOOK) You already did.
I love you.

                    EMILY
(ALL BUSINESS) Yes.

AS SHE CROSSES TO GET HER COAT... <u>SFX: KNOCK ON DOOR</u>.
ROSS GETS IT, <u>CHANDLER AND JOEY ENTER</u>.

                    JOEY
This city is amazing! We took the train
from the airport, and a taxi from the
train to the hotel!
                    ROSS
(BEAT) And...?

                    JOEY
It's all slightly different from the
stuff we have at home!

                    CHANDLER
(BEAT) No.

                    JOEY
(TO CHANDLER, BRIGHTLY) Hey, you want to
go sightseeing?

                    CHANDLER
I'm tired. I want to sleep.

Handwritten notes:

Hey, what are the bridesmaids wearing? It shouldn't be too traditional, right?

IS SHE TOO MUCH OF A BITCH? —D.C.

We want to SEE London, GUYS! K.B.

> Everyone I run into here in London has been so kind. It's really been a great experience for me. Everyone knows and watches the show and loves the characters. And the guy I play is very approachable, very down to earth.
> MATT LE BLANC

<u>"The One With Ross's Wedding"</u> FIRST DRAFT

                         JOEY
Too bad. You should have slept on the plane,
like I told you to.

                     CHANDLER
It was hard for me to sleep with you
constantly asking the stewardess, "Are we
there, yet?"

[handwritten: cut?]
[handwritten: No. IT'S SO JOEY]
[handwritten: YES.]

                            DISSOLVE TO: *[handwritten: No.]*

                     SCENE E
<u>EXT. LONDON STREET "A" - A BIT LATER</u> (DAY 3) MONICA,
ROSS AND EMILY ARE WALKING DOWN THE STREET.

                     ROSS
You're going to love Montgomery Hall.

                    EMILY
My parents got married there.

                   MONICA
It must be great if you're willing to
plan a whole wedding in three weeks,
just so you can have it there before
they tear it down.

                    ROSS
It really is the most beautiful
building you'll ever see.

THEY TURN THE CORNER AND SEE THAT THE HALL
HAS BEEN PARTIALLY DEMOLISHED. ALL THAT
REMAINS ARE MOST OF THE FOUR WALLS, AND A
PILE OF RUBBLE ON THE GROUND.

                    EMILY
Oh, my god.

                    ROSS
It's gone.

[handwritten: Move up in scene?]

AS THEY STAND THERE IN SHOCK, WE...FADE OUT.

               <u>END OF ACT ONE</u>

> "We realized that we wanted more jeopardy in the first act break and that the meaning wasn't really clear when the church was torn down. Ross and Emily could have just found another place. So we had Monica unwittingly convince Emily that she should postpone the wedding – which led to the fight between her and Ross and then the wedding being off at the act break.
> MICHAEL BORKOW

<u>"The One With Ross's Wedding"</u> FIRST DRAFT

<u>ACT TWO</u>

<u>SCENE H</u>

FADE IN: <u>EXT. RUBBLE - A FEW MINUTES LATER</u> (DAY 3)
(Monica, Ross, Emily, Construction Worker, Extras)
MONICA IS TALKING WITH A CONSTRUCTION WORKER. ROSS AND
EMILY ARE WHERE WE LEFT THEM.

                    EMILY
          I can't believe it's gone.

                    ROSS
          (COMFORTING) It's all right.

WHAT HAPPENED TO JOKES? - D.C.

                    EMILY
          (FREAKED) How is it all right?

                    ROSS
          (BEAT) Uh-huh, I see that. (THEN) Look, we
          just gotta keep getting stuff ready for the
          wedding like we were doing. We'll find
          another place.

                                        CUT TO:

<u>SCENE J</u>

<u>INT. MONICA & RACHEL'S APT. - SAME TIME</u> (DAY 3)
(Phoebe, Rachel) PHOEBE IS LYING ON THE COUCH, WORKING
ON HER GIFT. THEY LOOK A LITTLE MORE LIKE PUPPETS
NOW. RACHEL FLIPS THROUGH A CATALOGUE. PHOEBE HOLDS UP
THE PUPPETS.

                    PHOEBE
          What do you think? Does this one totally
          capture Ross, and does this one totally
          capture Emily?

What are we doing here?

                    RACHEL
          They kinda look the same to me.

Being funny?

                    PHOEBE
          (RE: ROSS AND EMILY) I know, those two <u>do</u>
          look like they could be related, don't they?

<u>"The One With Ross's Wedding"</u> FIRST DRAFT

> " In addition to Phoebe and the puppets, we originally had this scene where Rachel reupholsters the couch to get over Ross, but it just wasn't funny. This was at the end of the season and we're in the writers' room at five in the morning, and somebody says, 'What if she, like, reupholsters the couch?' When you haven't slept in two days, that really seems funny. Then you go see it and you go, 'Boy were we tired.' But I think cutting it is what made the 'London Baby' stuff with Joey evolve - which was hilarious. "
>
> GREG MALINS

RACHEL
You think they'd like a clock?

PHOEBE
Why don't you ask them. (HOLDS UP PUPPETS)
No, wait, don't. They don't have ears yet.

WHAT IS THIS REALLY ABOUT? WE MAY NEED MORE OF A STORY TO COMPETE W/ THE LONDON STUFF. ALTHOUGH, I DO LIKE PUPPETS

RACHEL FLIPS THROUGH THE CATALOGUE SOME MORE

PHOEBE (CON'T.)
(OFF PUPPETS) You know what I need? Velcro.
For the hands and lips, so they can hold
hands and kiss. And some here, for the
honeymoon.

MARTA, WHAT ABOUT AN ALL-PUPPET "FRIENDS"? DON'T REJECT THIS SO FAST.
— D.C.

CUT TO:

<u>SCENE K</u>

<u>SIGHTSEEING MONTAGE</u>: (Chandler, Joey, Man In Line,
Tourist, American #1, American #2, American #3, Taxi
Driver, Extras) <u>EXT. LONDON STREET "B" - THAT DAY</u>
(DAY 3) CHANDLER AND JOEY ARE WALKING DOWN THE
STREET.

CHANDLER
I'm exhausted. I don't want to do anything
else.

THEY PASS A GROUP OF PEOPLE WAITING IN LINE.

JOEY
Ooo, let's do this.
JOEY GETS IN LINE. CHANDLER RELUCTANTLY FOLLOWS.

They Came, They Saw, They Had A Ball!

Clockwise from top left: the crew gets into position to shoot Richard Branson in his scene with Matthew Perry and Matt Le Blanc; assistant director Ben Weiss backs up director Kevin Bright; she's funny too – Kevin Bright's wife Claudia entertains ICM boss Nancy Josephson, Courteney Cox, Robin Seigel and Greg Malins; Sarah Ferguson and Matt rehearse their scene; Ben Weiss watches over Matthew Perry; Scott Silveri, Francette Levangie and Michael Borkow head out to Matt Le Blanc's cast and crew party on their first night; Matthew Perry in racing gear with David Crane's assistant Adrienne Turner; Helen Baxendale takes a break; Matthew Perry with Todd Stevens and Matt Le Blanc at the racing track; Marta Kauffman and her son Sam Skloff; Kevin Bright and his two sons Zachary and Justin; Kevin Bright brings the script to life; writers/producers Scott Silveri and Shana Goldberg-Meehan in the writers' hotel work room.

<u>"The One With Ross's Wedding"</u> FIRST DRAFT

                        CHANDLER
What is it?   ← *LET MATHEW IMPROV HERE?*

                        JOEY
I don't know. But isn't it great?

                        CHANDLER
We're just standing in a line.   *WILL AMERICANS GET THIS? -D.C*

                        JOEY
No, we're not. We're standing in a queue.

                                    DISSOLVE TO:

"And then we'll make the pants really, really tight ..."
Costume designer Debra McGuire confers with
Matt Le Blanc on the Westminster Abbey set.

<u>"The One With Ross's Wedding"</u> FIRST DRAFT

<u>EXT. LONDON STREET "C" - A BIT LATER</u>. CHANDLER AND
JOEY ARE STILL IN LINE. JOEY SEES A TOURIST TAKING A
PICTURE OF TWO OTHER TOURISTS.

> JOEY (CON'T.)
> (TO GUY WITH CAMERA) Hey, get in that
> picture. I'll take one of all of you.

> TOURIST
> No. I don't know them. I'm taking a picture
> for them.

JOEY BACKS OFF. HE LOOKS OVER AND SEES CHANDLER
DRAPED ACROSS A STRANGER'S SHOULDER, ASLEEP.

> MAN IN LINE
> (TO JOEY) Will you please tell your friend
> I'm spoken for?

> > > DISSOLVE TO:

<u>INT. PUB - A BIT LATER</u>. IT'S PRETTY CROWDED. <u>JOEY AND
CHANDLER ENTER</u>.

> JOEY
> Check it out. An English pub.

> CHANDLER
> It's a bar. We have bars in America.

> JOEY
> (TO PASSERBY) How you doing? Joey Tribbiani,
> America.

THEY SEE A GROUP OF AMERICANS DRINKING NEARBY.

> AMERICAN #1
> (TO BARTENDER) Dude, another Bud Light.

> AMERICAN #2
> Me, too.

> AMERICAN #3
> Three Bud Lights.

> JOEY
> (SINCERE) Ah, merry old England.

> > > DISSOLVE TO:

> "London is just a really cool town. We've been having a blast. The major concern is not getting hit by cars!"
> MATTHEW PERRY

hate to do it but this has all gotta go.

<u>"The One With Ross's Wedding"</u> FIRST DRAFT

<u>EXT. LONDON MARRIOTT - A BIT LATER</u>. A TAXI PULLS UP
IN FRONT.

                                                    CUT TO:

<u>INT. TAXI - CONTINUOUS</u>. CHANDLER AND JOEY ARE IN THE
BACK OF THE TAXI. CHANDLER IS ASLEEP. JOEY GIVES THE
DRIVER SOME ~~MONEY~~.

ASK TODD ABOUT A DOUBLE-DECKER BUS INSTEAD

                    JOEY (CON'T.)
        Wake up, Chandler. We're there.

                    CHANDLER
        Wha—?

                    JOEY
        I can't believe you. That's one of the only
        times you'll be riding in a London taxi, and
        you missed the whole experience.

                    CHANDLER
        It's a taxi. It's just like what we do all
        the time, but on the other side of the road.

                    JOEY
        (HADN'T NOTICED) Oh, yeah... AS THEY GET OUT
        AND GO INTO THE MARRIOTT, WE...

haven't we pushed this to far?

WHAT'S YOUR POINT?

                                                    CUT TO:

                    <u>SCENE M</u>

<u>INT. DRESS SHOP - SAME TIME</u> (DAY 3) MONICA'S TRYING
ON HER BRIDESMAID DRESS. EMILY IS WITH HER, AND IS
EXTREMELY STRESSED OUT. THE SALESLADY IS PINNING IT.
AS THE SALESLADY STICKS THE NEXT PIN IN... *CUT?*

                    MONICA
        Ow!

                    SALESLADY
        Sorry. Good thing this dress is red.

                    EMILY
        (TO MONICA) Tell me the truth. Do you hate
        the dress?

Can't we just incorporate this into next scene?

<u>"The One With Ross's Wedding" FIRST DRAFT</u>

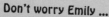

Don't worry Emily ...

... Monica loves the gown you've chosen for the bridesmaids – even though time constraints will eventually cause this nifty scene to be cut from the final shooting script.

YES, WE DO.
AT THE
WEDDING.
REMEMBER?

But then we don't get to see Courteney in her red dress

                    MONICA
(SINCERE) No, I think it looks great.
Wedding or no wedding, I'm wearing
this thing on Sunday.

EMILY REACTS.

              MONICA (CON'T.)
I'm kidding. I'm kidding. Of course,
there's going to be a wedding.

                    EMILY
Who knows? I mean any place nice will
have been booked for months.

                    MONICA
Look, worse comes to worse, and you
don't have the wedding right away, is
that <u>such</u> a bad thing? (THEN) I just
mean, maybe it was meant to happen.
Like it was a sign, or something. You
know, like, maybe you weren't <u>supposed</u>
to get married in that hall.

Let's just have EMILY tell Ross that MONICA said this in their next scene... okay?

Your Assignment: WRITE IT

<u>"The One With Ross's Wedding"</u> FIRST DRAFT

> EMILY
> Or maybe we're not supposed to get married.

> MONICA
> Exactly! (THEN) What?

> EMILY
> You're right. It's a sign. I have to go.

<u>EMILY EXITS</u>

> MONICA
> Emily! Wait!

MONICA STARTS TO FOLLOW EMILY, BUT GETS STUCK ON THE PIN THE SALESLADY IS STICKING IN.

> MONICA (CON'T.)
> Ow!

> SALESLADY
> You deserved that one.

> DISSOLVE TO:

<u>SCENE P</u>

<u>INT. CHANDLER & JOEY'S HOTEL ROOM - THAT EVENING</u>
(NIGHT 3) (Chandler, Joey, Monica, Ross) CHANDLER'S COLLAPSED ON HIS BED, BAGS STILL PACKED. JOEY'S UNPACKING.

> JOEY
> I love London. Check it out. They even put the phone on the left side of the bed instead of the right.

> CHANDLER
> There's no rule, Joey.

> JOEY
> Of course not. They don't need a rule. This place is all about custom and traditions.

overkill?

Strictly between us, she's cuter than Venus. And what's more she's got arms. Courteney Cox pauses during the bridal shop scene.

"The One With Ross's Wedding" FIRST DRAFT

SFX: KNOCK ON DOOR. JOEY OPENS IT. IT'S MONICA. THE
GUYS AD-LIB HELLOS. SHE ENTERS, CONCERNED AND
DISTRACTED, AND JUST STANDS THERE IN THE MIDDLE OF
THE ROOM.

JOEY (CON'T.)
You okay?

MONICA
Uh-huh.

CHANDLER
What's wrong?

MONICA
I don't know how it happened.

IS THIS MY JOKE?

JOEY
Oh. I know what's going on. (COMFORTING) It
happens to everybody. They have no business
putting it there. It's called a bidet.

MONICA
I think I sorta, kinda...convinced Emily
that she shouldn't marry Ross. I was trying
to comfort her. And I don't think I did.
(THEN) Ross is gonna kill me. I'm gonna kill
me.

FX: KNOCK ON DOOR. CHANDLER OPENS IT. ROSS ENTERS,
UPSET.

ROSS
Emily wants to call off the wedding.
She says the building being demolished
is a "sign". (THEN) Why would she say
something like that?

HE SHOULD KNOW ALREADY + COME IN PISSED

MONICA
Maybe she talked to someone. Like me.

ROSS
Like some friend of hers who's single
and really bitter about it?

MONICA
(A BIT ANNOYED) No, me. Actually me. She
talked to me.

> Sometimes we have Joey jokes
> that are incredibly funny but we
> end up pulling them because we've
> just got too many and it's overkill.
> The bidet joke in the table draft of
> Ross's Wedding was one dumb
> Joey joke too many, and anyway,
> nobody's that dumb.
>
> MICHAEL BORKOW

"The One With Ross's Wedding" FIRST DRAFT

ROSS TURNS AND STARES AT HER. AFTER A TENSE MOMENT...

> CHANDLER
> I gonna go to the bathroom.

HE EXITS TO THE BATHROOM.

> JOEY
> Me, too.

HE, TOO, EXITS TO THE BATHROOM.

> ROSS
> What?

> MONICA
> I'm sorry. I'm so sorry. She was upset about
> the building, and I told her that you
> weren't gonna have marigolds, but maybe you
> could, you know, if you didn't have
> to...rush into it.

> ROSS
> You told her you thought we were rushing
> into it? From now on, when you're thinking
> something like that...run it by me!

HE STARTS FOR THE DOOR.

> MONICA
> Where are you going?

> ROSS
> Emily took her parents to see what's left of
> the hall.

HE STARTS FOR THE DOOR. SHE FOLLOWS.

> MONICA
> I'm coming with you.

THEY EXIT. AFTER A MOMENT, THE BATHROOM DOOR OPENS.
CHANDLER AND JOEY WALK OUT.

> CHANDLER
> Pretty intense.

> “My fantasy is that Joey and Chandler finally get together. Ross and Phoebe take their kids and move to the country. Rachel and Monica start dating, fall in love and realize they've had it with men.”
> COURTENEY COX

DO WE NEED TO TAKE BOTTLED WATER TO ENGLAND?

Why?

<u>"The One With Ross's Wedding"</u> FIRST DRAFT

                    JOEY
        Hey, throw me the remote. Let's
        watch some British TV.

CHANDLER TOSSES HIM THE REMOTE.

                    JOEY (CON'T.)
        And tonight, we can order some fish and
        chips from room service. I'm loving this
        country. I'm telling you, I could live here.

JOEY TURNS ON THE TV. <u>SFX: THE "CHEERS" THEME SONG</u>

                    CHANDLER
        (PLEASANTLY SURPRISED) Hey!

                    JOEY
        They must know there's Americans staying in
        this room.

THEY SIT DOWN, EACH ON HIS OWN BED, TO WATCH THE
SHOW. THE LYRICS START. AS THE SONG CONTINUES, JOEY
GETS SADDER AND SADDER. SOON, CHANDLER NOTICES.

                    CHANDLER
        You okay?

                    JOEY
        (NOT CONVINCING) Uh-huh.

                                            CUT TO:

                  SCENE R

<u>INT. MONICA & RACHEL'S APT. - DAY, SAME TIME</u> (DAY 3)
(Phoebe, Rachel) PHOEBE'S LYING ON THE COUCH, WORKING
ON THE PUPPETS, WHICH NOW LOOK A LOT MORE LIKE ROSS
AND EMILY. <u>SFX: KEY JIGGLING IN LOCK</u>

                    PHOEBE
        (CALLING) Rachel?!

                    RACHEL (O.S.)
        My key's stuck.

                    PHOEBE
        I'm coming.

Handwritten annotations:

How ABOUT

JOEY
I HOPE ROSS DIDN'T THINK WE WENT IN THE BATHROOM BECAUSE WE WERE UNCOMFORTABLE WATCHING THEM ARGUE. AND THEN CHANDLER

(BEAT) I HOPE HE DID.

Can we get this?
ALL YOU NEED IS BUCKS.

tighten

<u>"The One With Ross's Wedding" FIRST DRAFT</u>

PHOEBE TRIES TO GET UP. SHE'S A BIT LIKE A TURTLE
LYING IN ITS SHELL, AND CAN'T QUITE GET OFF HER BACK.

> (PHOEBE (CON'T.)
> One second!

SHE ROCKS A LITTLE BIT, TRYING TO GET MOMENTUM TO
ROLL OVER. SHE HAS TO ROCK BACK AND FORTH SEVERAL
TIMES. JUST AS SHE MANAGES TO ROLL ONTO HER SIDE AND
THEN SIT UP, <u>RACHEL ENTERS</u>, CARRYING A SHOPPING BAG.

> RACHEL
> (CHEERY) Wrong key. Don't get up. (RE:BAG) I
> found it. The perfect gift.

> PHOEBE
> Show me, show me. (RE: PUPPETS) But wait,
> they shouldn't see it, yet. (puts them face
> down) Okay.

> RACHEL
> (PULLING IT OUT OF BAG) Ta-da!

> PHOEBE
> (BEAT) What is it?

> RACHEL
> What does it look like?

> PHOEBE
> Like some kind of...crystal...tennis ball.

> RACHEL
> Exactly! It's expensive, so it's clear I
> care. But it has no special significance.
> (THEN) Think they'll like it?

> PHOEBE
> Well... You know what? I just think it's
> great you're getting them anything. I mean,
> if I were in love with a guy and he was
> getting married...

*Phoebe is not
stupid. She just
has a different
point of reference
for everything.*
LISA KUDROW

*HAVE MORE
FUN W/ THIS
SCENE.
—D.C.*

*Let's cut to
the chase*

<u>"The One With Ross's Wedding"</u> FIRST DRAFT

> RACHEL
> What? I'm not in love with Ross.

> PHOEBE
> What do you mean?

> RACHEL
> I'm not in love with him.

PHOEBE LOOKS CONFUSED FOR A BEAT. THEN...

> PHOEBE
> Oh, I get it. (TO ROSS PUPPET) She's not in love with you. I was just kidding. She didn't go to your wedding because she has lots of work to do. (AS ROSS PUPPET) Oh. Okay. That's what I figured.

LISA IS HILARIOUS HERE ↗

I KNOW, BUT WE'VE GOTTA CUT IT.

Get it straight! Rachel is NOT in love with Ross.

47

<u>"The One With Ross's Wedding"</u> FIRST DRAFT

                    RACHEL
    I'm not going to the wedding because he's my
    ex-boyfriend. It'd be uncomfortable. It's
    not like I'm not going because if I were
    there, I'd be thinking, "Why is he marrying
    her instead of me?". Or, like, "I should,
    you know, be up there, instead of her." You
    know? (THEN) Oh, my god. I still love him,
    don't I?

MORE MORE MORE

                    PHOEBE
    Oh, sweetheart, you didn't know?

                    RACHEL
    Why didn't you tell me?

Love it — but can we say it?

                    PHOEBE
    We thought you knew. It's so obvious.
    Or, like, you know, "Monica likes things
    clean or "Hey, Joey, you're gay.".

                    RACHEL
    What???

Why couldn't Monica (AKA Greg Mronde) decorate what's left of the hall with flowers. candles. etc. — to change Emily's mind?

                                        CUT TO:
                        SCENE 1

    <u>EXT. RUBBLE - THAT NIGHT</u> (NIGHT 3) (Monica, Ross,
    Emily, Steven Waltham, Andrea Waltham) EMILY'S PARENTS
    ARE SEARCHING THROUGH THE RUBBLE WITH FLASHLIGHTS.
    MONICA AND ROSS APPROACH.

                    ROSS
    There they are.

                    MONICA
    Okay, now things are gonna work
    out for you guys.

    EMILY'S PARENTS COME OVER. AD-LIB HELLOS.

                    ROSS
    Is Emily here?

                    STEVEN WALTHAM
    She's around back.

<u>"The One With Ross's Wedding"</u> FIRST DRAFT

ANDREA WALTHAM
We carved our initials on a
wooden beam the night we got
married here. We were hoping
to find them.

Do WE NEED?

MONICA
Any luck?

STEVEN WALTHAM
No. (SHOWING IT) But we did
find a tile from the bathroom
counter.

ROSS
Why would you want that?

ANDREA AND STEVEN SHARE AN AWKWARD LOOK.

STEVEN WALTHAM
Mrs. Waltham, uh...sat there once.

ROSS AND MONICA REACT. <u>EMILY COMES OVER</u>.

— lets just lose the Walthams here?

ANDREA WALTHAM
Well, we're going to be on our way.

<u>THEY</u> AD-LIB GOODBYES AND <u>EXIT</u>. ROSS APPROACHES EMILY.

ROSS
So, about what happened today...

START SCENE HERE

MONICA
(STEPS FORWARD) Look, yours is probably going
to take a lot longer than mine. So, if I could
just jump in for a sec. Emily, never listen to
me. I'm a stupid, horrible idiot. And I'd make
a great sister-in-law. (THEN) Okay.

SHE CROSSES AWAY, BUT STAYS WITHIN EARSHOT.

ROSS
So, still thinking you don't want to get
married?

For DAVID CRANE

Date _____ Time _____ A.M. P.M.

WHILE YOU WERE OUT

M MARTA KAUFFMAN

Of _____

☐ Phone _____
☐ Fax _____
☐ Mobile _____

	Area Code	Number	Extension
TELEPHONED	✓	PLEASE CALL	✓
CAME TO SEE YOU	✓	WILL CALL AGAIN	
WANTS TO SEE YOU	✓	URGENT	
RETURNED YOUR CALL		SPECIAL ATTENTION	✓

Message Are you sitting down? We got Jennifer Saunders & Tom Conti for Mr. & Mrs. Waltham! You can stand up now. Yay!

Signed

The Friends Meet The (British) Press

*O*nce they had recovered somewhat from their jet-lag, the cast and producers agreed to a press conference at Channel 4. The network took the precaution of erecting barriers outside its offices to protect the arriving cast. "But not a single fan braved the pouring rain to get a glimpse of the actors," *The Times* gloated the following day, "and the numerous police officers, waiting to control the surging crowds, had to twiddle their thumbs." But as it happens, the city's thousands of *Friends* fans were unaware that the event was taking place. Once word about where the location sites were to be was broad-

"What do you care what I sleep in?" Matthew Perry volleys smartly with the press.

cast on several radio stations the next day, it was all the police could do to keep the crowds from swarming all over the set. Several days later, the *Daily News* reported that "police had a job keeping the crowd numbering thousands of tourists and workers in check" as Matthew Perry and Matt Le Blanc filmed a scene with Virgin Airlines boss Richard Branson. And two studio audiences numbering around 400 each stood in the rain for hours at the Fountain

Yes, it's true: her Friends contract prohibits her from cutting or bleaching her hair.

"There was a helicopter circling over my house. Then my publicist called at the crack of dawn and said, 'Are you ready for this? You're supposed to be dead from a drug overdose.' No one was more shocked than me. I walked outside and the story ended. Then I called my mother and told her I wasn't dead. I'm not the guy the tabloids paint me to be. I don't have enough time in my schedule to have all these addictions. But being dead was the worst. I hated that."
                    MATT LE BLANC

Studios in Wembley for a chance to see the cast members in the flesh.

Meanwhile, back in the press conference, the show's co-creator Marta Kauffman found the assembled British journalists to be more reserved than their American counterparts (although you'd never know it from what they wrote), and yet one or two – who were described the next day in a rival column as "tabloid scum in pervs' raincoats" – did attempt to probe Jennifer Aniston's love life. (Unsuccessfully, as it turned out.) Even so, cheeky questions were not the order of the

Go ahead. Ask them anything: David Schwimmer, Matt Le Blanc, Matthew Perry, Kevin Bright, Channel 4's Stuart Cosgrove, David Crane, Marta Kauffman, Courteney Cox and Jennifer Aniston.

day. The queries were more on the order of the, "What's your favourite TV show," kind-of-thing.

The press was kind and the fans were adorable. As with their preceding visit to England, the stars of Friends were wowed by the warmth of the London reception and they spent both their days and nights interacting with fans in a way they wouldn't dream of back home. And they did something they have mostly refrained from in America of late – they made themselves available for interviews and photo shoots.

As the filming continued, more and more rumours about the episode's plotline began to circulate – most of them completely off the mark. The Sun in a "telly exclusive" was the first to, they claimed, reveal the show's storyline. ROSS WEDS RACHEL the headline proclaimed. Well, uh, no fellas – not really. Nice try, though. Another screamed ROSS JILTS EMILY AT THE ALTAR! Sorry guys, wrong again. Even the studio audiences who

attended the filming would be kept in the dark as to the real outcome. Although the producers didn't really shoot three endings as they hinted they would in pre-show interviews, they evacuated the studio audience before filming the real ending. Ultimately, the subterfuge and frenzied speculation confused everything to such an extent that, while one or two accurate accounts of the episode did eventually make their way into the newspapers, no one could be sure which version was on the mark. And that, of course, was just the way the mischief-makers at Friends had intended it all along.

Friends double bluff to keep fans guessing

"The One With Ross's Wedding" FIRST DRAFT

                    EMILY
It's all so rushed. I don't know what I
want.

                    ROSS
It's okay. We don't have to get married.

                    EMILY
(PULLED UP SHORT) Oh.

                    ROSS
We're only doing this because you want to
get married (INDICATING THE PILE OF RUBBLE)
here. And I gotta tell you, I don't know if
that's such a priority any more.
EMILY SMILES.

                ROSS (CON'T.)
We can get married five years from now, for
all I care. As long as we're together.

STET
AS IS

                    EMILY
You really mean it, don't you?
You're absolutely positive we're
meant for each other.

                    ROSS
If I weren't, I wouldn't be
standing in the rubble of a
demolished dance hall three
thousand miles from home.

*let's get some
David physical
business in here
somewhere —*

                    MONICA
(LEANS IN) And neither would I.
(THEN) Sorry.
                    ROSS
It sucks that we can't get married
where you wanted. But I'd marry you
right here in this rubble. I'd
marry you in whatever is going to
be built on top of this rubble.

                    EMILY
I believe it's to be a sewage
treatment plant.

Bright Kauffman Crane

> talk to Kevin re:
casting
> find out about
tours for kids
> get more film
> proof rewrite
> get raincoat!!
> new dividers for
extra scenes
> write scenes
for 1st episode
next season

MARTA KAUFFMAN

<u>"The One With Ross's Wedding"</u> FIRST DRAFT

> ROSS
> Look, I'm just making a point, here. It
> doesn't matter. (TAKES HER HAND) <u>This</u> is
> what matters.

> EMILY
> Then let's do it.

> ROSS
> Yeah?

> EMILY
> Yeah.

> ROSS
> All right. First thing tomorrow, we decide
> on a new place.

> EMILY
> No. Here. Like you said. We'll do it in the
> rubble.

HE SMILES, THEN KISSES HER. THEN...

> MONICA
> This is going to be so romantic. (TO EMILY)
> Do you like tall skinny candles, or shorter,
> fatter ones?

> EMILY
> (GAZING AT HIM) It doesn't matter.

SHE KISSES HIM. AS THEY KISS...

> MONICA
> It kinda does, 'cause I can get them first
> thing in the morning.

AS THEY CONTINUE TO KISS, WE...

CUT TO:

<u>SCENE W</u>

<u>INT. CHANDLER & JOEY'S HOTEL ROOM - EARLY THE NEXT</u>
<u>MORNING</u> (DAY 4) (Chandler, Joey) JOEY'S AWAKE, TOSSING
AND TURNING. CHANDLER'S FAST ASLEEP. JOEY GETS UP AND
CROSSES TO CHANDLER.

> JOEY
> (NUDGING HIM) Chandler. Chandler.

We've got to cut this scene by a half.

<u>"The One With Ross's Wedding"</u> FIRST DRAFT

                    CHANDLER
(WAKES UP) Hey.

                    JOEY
Do you feel...weird at all?

                    CHANDLER
Uh-uh.

                    JOEY
You don't feel something in
your stomach?

                    CHANDLER
Joey, are you homesick?

                    JOEY
Yeah, I think I just might be.

                    CHANDLER
Well, what do you want to do?

                    JOEY
I don't know. I'd call you at home, but
you're here.

                    CHANDLER
(THINKS A BEAT) All right. Come with me.

                                    SMASH CUT TO:

> "With the scene with Chandler and Joey at the London McDonalds we just realized we could get (Joey's homesickness) across in one scene where Joey watches TV and gets sad over the *Cheers* theme. You didn't need to do three hits of it, you got it all in one."
> GREG MALINS

too Saccharine (or whatever that word is.)
↑
you mean sucky?

Sometimes even they have to laugh at the things they say. Matthew Perry and Matt Le Blanc had to re-do this scene three times before they could nail it without breaking up.

<u>"The One With Ross's Wedding"</u> FIRST DRAFT

<u>SCENE X</u>

<u>EXT. LONDON STREET "D" - A BIT LATER</u> (DAY 4) (Joey, Chandler, Extras) CLOSE ON: JOEY'S EXCITED FACE BASKING IN A YELLOW LIGHT. PULL BACK TO REVEAL THAT JOEY AND CHANDLER ARE LOOKING UP AT THE GOLDEN ARCHES OF MCDONALD'S.

CUT TO:

An interim rewrite of the script called for Chandler and Joey to do some sightseeing around London on a double-decker bus. But this scenic interlude was scrapped following the happy addition of Sarah Ferguson and Richard Branson cameos. Here Matthew Perry and Matt Le Blanc have entirely too much fun for people who are supposed to be working. The high-priced extras in the background are Marta Kauffman and Adam Chase.

"The One With Ross's Wedding" FIRST DRAFT

SCENE Y
INT. MCDONALD'S - MOMENTS LATER CHANDLER AND JOEY ARE
AT THE COUNTER.

                    CHANDLER
          See, just like home.

                    JOEY
          Yeah.
THE CASHIER HANDS HIM HIS TRAY. JOEY SMILES.

                    CASHIER
          (HEAVY COCKNEY ACCENT) Would
          you like some vinegar with your
          chips?

JOEY REACTS, CRESTFALLEN.
                    JOEY
          (TO CHANDLER) It's not the same
          at all.

                                        CUT TO:

SCENE Z

INT. ROSS'S HOTEL SUITE - SAME TIME
(DAY 4) ROSS AND EMILY ARE IN BED.
ROSS IS AWAKE.

                    ROSS
          (GENTLY) Em. Em, are you up?

                    EMILY
          Uh-huh.
SHE ROLLS OVER, TO FACE HIM.

                    ROSS
          We're getting married tomorrow.

                    EMILY
          (PLEASED) I know.
SHE KISSES HIM.

                    ROSS
          And, you know what? So, they
          knocked down the hall. Every
          wedding's gotta have one thing go
          wrong. Now we know what it is.

KEVIN BRIGHT'S TO DO LIST	
March 25, 11998	
9:00	Pick up at Marriott
10:00	Cast press conference
11:00	Table read
12:30	Production meeting
2:00	Location scout
6:00	Return to hotel
8:00	Dine w/ all Zen Central
March 26, 1998	
8:00	Pick up/ to Fountain Studios
9:30	Cast rehearsal
5:00	Producer run-through
8:30	Dine Karen, Deb & lads
March 27, 1998	
5:00	Pick up at hotel
6:00	1st location: Westminster A.
7:00	Return to hotel
8:00	Watch casting tape w Marta
March 28, 1998	
7:00	Location #1 Marriott Hotel
8:00	Shoot at #1 location
10:30	Company to 2nd location
11:00	Car for Claudia & kids
1:00	Lunch
2:00	Shoot at 2nd location
11:00	To hotel
March 29, 1998 Day off!!!!	
10:00	Car pick up
12:00	Lego village
6:00	Grease
9:00	Dine English Gardens
March 30, 1998	
8:00	Car pick up
9:30	Cast rehearses; Fountain Studio
2:00	Cast rehearsal
4:00	Network run-through
6:45	Car pick up – hotel
8:45	Kevin, Marta, David review tape
March 31, 1998	
6:00	Car pick up to Fountain Studio
9:00	Camera blocking
2:30	Lunch
3:30	Camera blocking
April 1, 1998	
7:30	Pick up at hotel
11:00	Refresh camera
5:00	Shoot 1st show w/ audience
11:00	Preshoot episode #501
April 2, 1998	
9:00	Car pick up
10:30	Crane rehearsal
12:30	Shoot show #2 w/ audience
8:00	Shoot show #3 w/ audience
April 3, 1998	
Wrap show !!!!!!	

<u>"The One With Ross's Wedding" FIRST DRAFT</u>

AS THEY KISS AGAIN, WE...   SMASH CUT TO:

<u>SCENE ZZ</u>

<u>INT. MONICA & RACHEL'S APT. - THE NEXT DAY</u> PHOEBE IS
LYING ON THE COUCH. <u>RACHEL ENTERS</u>.

> RACHEL
> I'm going to London.

> PHOEBE
> What?

do we get to fly first class to London?

> RACHEL
> Don't forget to feed their birds.

> PHOEBE
> What do you mean, you're going to London?

> RACHEL
> I have to tell Ross I love him. (THEN) You
> take care. Don't have the babies till I get
> back.

Kisses her belly?

SHE BLOWS PHOEBE A KISS AND STARTS FOR THE DOOR.

> PHOEBE
> But Ross loves Emily.

> RACHEL
> I know. I just think he should know
> exactly how I feel. He deserves to have
> all the information.

> PHOEBE *(PANICKY)*
> But he's happy. They're happy. This is a
> terrible idea.

PHOEBE TRIES TO GET UP, ROCKING BACK AND FORTH.

> PHOEBE (CON'T.)
> Rachel, wait. Rachel!

are we staying late tonight?

> RACHEL
> Bye.

WHAT do you call late?

> "It's weird, the cast of *Friends* are almost closer to me than my own family.
> JENNIFER ANISTON

"The One With Ross's Wedding" FIRST DRAFT

RACHEL EXITS. PHOEBE CAN'T GET UP. STILL ROCKING...

> PHOEBE
> Rachel, don't go! (TO BELLY, ANGRY) Work
> with me here!

SHE GIVES UP. THEN...

> PHOEBE (CON'T.)
> (CALLING) Rachel! I need a hug!

END OF ACT TWO   FADE OUT.

The One Where Johnny Makes Friends

It was unprecedented really. They hadn't done it in years. Well, not together anyway. Yes, all six of the Friends granted an exclusive one-on-one television interview with Johnny Vaughan during the filming of "The One with Ross's Wedding". Not that it was easy. Everything about the episode was very hush-hush, so Johnny had to agree to stay locked up in a dressing room between meetings. And that, admittedly, was nerve-racking. And boring. And he never knew when he was going to be summoned and for which star. But those were the rules and he took them like a man – without too much whimpering anyway.

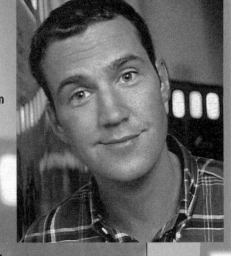

Johnny understood that because he had only one day on the set "to bond" with the cast, there was going to have to be "a lot of sucking up", so he brought gifts for everyone. A personally signed Barry Manilow LP for Matthew Perry; a book of poetry for the sensitive David Schwimmer; guitar strings for the non-guitar-playing Lisa Kudrow; a fussy ceramic thingy for Courteney Cox; a can of paint for one-time carpenter Matt Le Blanc; and a Senegal bushbaby adoption certificate from the London Zoo for Jennifer Aniston. Actually, the gifts didn't go over all that well – with the exception of Jennifer's monkey, but hey, it got the ball rolling. Sort of.

In fact, the cast (including Lisa Kudrow – who talked to Johnny by telephone) made some really unusual revelations to Johnny; Matthew said that the cast is a "sickeningly likeable bunch", and that "there isn't a jerk in the group". Courteney Cox admitted that she makes things up about the similarities about her and Monica depending on how bored she is with an interview; Matt said that he has no choice but to keep his cool with the girls because "they won't give it up"; Jennifer told him about her personal skin care regime; David tried (unsuccessfully) to teach him to be humble; and Lisa told him that he was scaring her. Yes, you could say that the cast's revelations added significantly to Friends lore. (It wouldn't be true. But you could.) And Johnny had fun too. Admittedly, he was escorted to and from interviews by scary security guards and one or two times things got a little ugly when he got busted sneaking a peek at the rehearsals. But all in all, it was an historical occasion. For Johnny anyway.

<u>"The One With Ross's Wedding"</u> FIRST DRAFT

<u>ACT THREE</u>

<u>SCENE A</u>

FADE IN:
<u>INT. WALTHAM'S RESIDENCE - LONDON/MONICA & RACHEL'S</u>
<u>APT. - NIGHT/DAY</u> (NIGHT 3/DAY 3) <u>(Phoebe, Housekeeper)</u>
WE SEE A WALL OF EMILY'S PARENTS' HOUSE. THERE IS A
TELEPHONE. IT RINGS. A <u>HOUSEKEEPER ENTERS</u> AND ANSWERS.

> HOUSEKEEPER
> Waltham residence.

<u>INTERCUT WITH:</u> <u>INT. MONICA & RACHEL'S APT. - SAME</u>
<u>TIME</u>. PHOEBE IS FRANTIC.

> PHOEBE
> Yes. Is this Emily's parents' house?

What's Lisa doing here?

> HOUSEKEEPER
> Young lady, that is not how one addresses a
> person when calling. First one identifies
> oneself, and then politely asks for the
> party.

> PHOEBE
> What?! What are you saying?!

> HOUSEKEEPER
> Now let's try this again, shall we?

THE MAID HANGS UP.

> PHOEBE
> Ugh!

PHOEBE HITS REDIAL.

> HOUSEKEEPER
> Waltham residence.

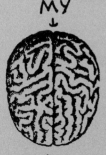

MY ↓

IS BROKEN

MUST HAVE CHOCOLATE

> PHOEBE
> WITH ENGLISH ACCENT) Yes, hello. This is
> Phoebe Buffay. I was wondering, <u>please</u>, if
> it's not too much trouble, <u>please</u>, if I
> might speak with Emily Waltham, <u>please</u>.

<u>*"The One With Ross's Wedding"* FIRST DRAFT</u>

HOUSEKEEPER
She's at the rehearsal dinner. Goodbye.

PHOEBE
No, wait. I'll be nice. I just need the
number for where they are. I just need to
tell somebody that somebody realized that
they loved somebody. And that somebody just
left for London to do this really stupid,
idiotic thing that could embarrass herself
and ruin the whole wedding!

2A

HOUSEKEEPER
I'm afraid I stopped listening at the third
"somebody". But thank you for calling.

(ALT. WITH
"BUM")

PHOEBE
Look, lady, if you don't give me that
number, I'm going to come over there and
kick your snooty ass all the way to... New
Glouken... shire! (THEN) Hello? Hello?

CUT TO:

<u>SCENE B</u>

<u>INT. RESTAURANT - LONDON - SAME TIME</u>
ROSS AND EMILY ARE GREETING PEOPLE AS THEY ARRIVE FOR
THE REHEARSAL DINNER. A WOMAN APPROACHES THEM.

EMILY
(SOTTO) My cousin Jane, you met her at my
parents house. ROSS (SOTTO) Like or don't
like?

EMILY
(SOTTO) Like.

ROSS/EMILY
(GREETING HER WARMLY) Hello. How are you?
So glad you could come.

— Don't cut
this!

AN OLDER COUPLE APPROACHES THEM.
ROSS
(SOTTO) Uncle Charles and Aunt Elizabeth.

<u>"The One With Ross's Wedding"</u> FIRST DRAFT

EMILY

.(SOTTO) Like or don't like?

ROSS

(SOTTO) Don't like.

ROSS/EMILY

(EXACT SAME TONE) Hello. How are you? So glad you could come.

WHY???

<u>JACK AND JUDY ENTER WITH MONICA</u>. AD-LIB HELLOS.

ROSS

Any trouble getting here?

JACK GELLER

Nah. (THEN) You know that Big Ben's not so big. We have clocks that big at home. We just don't make a fuss about it.

LAME
WHAT'S YOUR POINT?

MONICA

You don't need to tell anyone else, Dad.
STEVEN AND ANDREA WALTHAM COME OVER.

STEVEN WALTHAM

Hello, Gellers.

ANDREA WALTHAM

Quite a night.

JUDY GELLER

You did a beautiful job.

STEVEN WALTHAM

On that front, thank you again for going halves on everything with us. It's really quite generous of you.

JACK GELLER

Forget about it. The hell with tradition. We're happy to do it.

MEANWHILE, ACROSS THE ROOM, A WAITER IS OFFERING JOEY AND CHANDLER A TRAY OF HORS D'OEUVRES.

<u>"The One With Ross's Wedding"</u> FIRST DRAFT

                    JOEY
What's in it?

                    WAITER
Goat cheese, watercress and pancetta.

                    JOEY
(TO CHANDLER, UPSET) That's not right.   *— WILL BRITS*
Nothing's good here. I miss real food. Like   *UNDERSTAND?*
pigs-in-a-blanket and taquitos. I want to go
home. I miss my family. I miss the coffee
house. I miss ice.

too   *What would you prefer?*
mean   CHANDLER   *Steak and kidney pie?*
M.   Will you please stop whining and try to
         enjoy yourself?

JOEY STARES AT CHANDLER FOR A BEAT. THEN...

                    JOEY
(UPSET) You're different here, too. You're
mean in England.

MEANWHILE, ACROSS THE ROOM, JACK IS STILL TALKING WITH
STEVEN WALTHAM.

                    JACK GELLER
So, anytime you want to settle up, just let
me know what my half is.

                    STEVEN WALTHAM
Actually, I happen to have an accounting
right here.

                    JACK GELLER
Oh, please. I don't want to hear another
word about it.

JACK GIVES HIM A JOVIAL SLAP ON THE BACK. MR. WALTHAM
MOVES OFF. JACK SITS AT A TABLE TO STUDY THE BILL.
IT'S SEVERAL PAGES LONG.

                    JACK GELLER (CON'T.)
What the hell...?

<u>"The One With Ross's Wedding" FIRST DRAFT</u>

That's what you get for trying to be nice. Judy and Jack get their first look at the Waltham's breakdown of their share of the wedding expenses.

MONICA

What's the matter, Dad?

JACK GELLER

This bill for the wedding. There's got to be some kind of mistake.

ROSS

You're probably just confused 'cause it's pounds, which means it's...twice as much in dollars.

JACK GELLER

(READING BILL) Re-carpet first floor? New tiles in guest bath? Landscaping?

EMILY COMES OVER, CONCERNED.

"The One With Ross's Wedding" FIRST DRAFT

EMILY
Is everything all right?

Let's move this down cause it'll give Emily a chance to see Rachel

ROSS
(MOVING HER AWAY) Everything's fine.
I like your hair this way. What do
you call it?

EMILY
(BEAT) Up.

do we really want that? Wouldn't she immediately know something was up?

HE GIVES HER A KISS AND RETURNS TO HIS PARENTS.

JACK GELLER
Do you know he's asking us to buy him new
patio furniture!? I could use new patio
furniture!

JUDY GELLER
Jack, don't make a scene

Elliott is great with this

JACK GELLER
I'm not making a scene. He's making a scene.
I'm paying for the scene. (THEN) I'm gonna
give that son-of-a-bitch a piece of my mind.

ROSS
Dad, please. I don't want anything to upset
Emily tonight. Let me talk to him.

ROSS TAKES THE BILL AND STARTS OFF. JACK CALLS AFTER:

JACK GELLER
Ask him what automatic sprinklers have to do
with a wedding?!

CUT TO:

SCENE C

INT. AIRPORT TICKET COUNTER - AFTERNOON (DAY 3)
(Rachel, Ticket Agent, Person In Line, Extras)
RACHEL IS WAITING IN LINE AT THE CROWDED TICKET
COUNTER.SHE TURNS TO THE PERSON IN FRONT OF HER.

"The One With Ross's Wedding" FIRST DRAFT

                    RACHEL
Excuse me. Would you mind if I went ahead of
you? I have to get to London to tell someone
I love him.

                PERSON IN LINE
    (SERIOUS) I'm going to my mother's funeral. *too bitchy*

But she lets
him go ahead
                    RACHEL   *even for*
    (TAKEN ABACK) Oh, god. I'm sorry. That must   *Rachel*
be so — (THEN, NOTICING) Ooh, it's open!
It's open! Go! Go!

Can you believe it? Rachel is even more impossible in this draft
than in the final London shooting script. Here she pushes past a
man in the ticket line who's going home for his mother's funeral.

SHE SHOVES THE PERSON TOWARD THE OPEN AGENT. ANOTHER
AGENT QUICKLY OPENS UP, AND RACHEL RUNS OVER.

                 TICKET AGENT
    (EXTREMELY CHEERFUL) Hello!

                    RACHEL
    (EQUALLY CHEERFULLY) Hello! (THEN, FRANTIC)
When is your next flight to London?

"The One With Ross's Wedding" FIRST DRAFT

                    TICKET AGENT
There's one leaving in thirty minutes, but
I'm afraid it may be full. There's another
at eleven.

                    RACHEL
Please, you've got to get me on the
first one. I have to get to London to
tell someone I love him.

                    TICKET AGENT
(TOUCHED) Aww. Let me see what I can do.

I hear we're huge in England.

                    RACHEL
Thank you. Thank you. Thank you.

                    TICKET AGENT
(CHECKING COMPUTER) The last-minute fare.

Do you think it'll get us laid?

            TICKET AGENT (CON'T.)
on this ticket is twenty-seven hundred
dollars.

WE'RE NOT THAT HUGE.

                    RACHEL
Oh. How 'bout six hundred?

THE TICKET AGENT SHAKES HER HEAD.

                    RACHEL (CON'T.)
Six hundred and these earrings?

                    TICKET AGENT
They prefer if I don't barter.

                    RACHEL
It's just I don't have that much
left on my credit card.

                    TICKET AGENT
You can split it with another credit card.

                    RACHEL
How 'bout five cards?

<u>"The One With Ross's Wedding"</u> FIRST DRAFT

RACHEL HANDS OVER FIVE CARDS. THE AGENT STARTS
PROCESSING THEM.

TICKET AGENT (CON'T.)
I'm just going to need to see your passport.

RACHEL REACTS. OBVIOUSLY, SHE'S FORGOTTEN HER
PASSPORT.

RACHEL
(CHUMMY) Oh, you don't need to see that.
The picture's not very good. I have my
driver's license...and (WITH A WINK) a
twenty?

ON THE TICKET AGENT'S IMPASSIVE STARE, WE..
CUT TO:

Are you kidding? we can get pizza delivered to the moon.

Can we get pizza delivered to the Stage?

<u>SCENE D</u>

<u>INT. RESTAURANT - LONDON - LATER</u> (NIGHT 3)
(Ross, Steven Waltham, Extras) ROSS APPROACHES
MR. WALTHAM WHO'S CHATTING WITH SOME GUESTS.
ROSS
Mr. Waltham? Can I speak with you for a
second? (PULLING HIM ASIDE) Um, I happened
to glance at that bill you gave my father...

STEVEN WALTHAM
Oh, he shouldn't have shown you that. Let
the parents worry about what it costs.

HE STARTS TO MOVE OFF. ROSS PURSUES HIM.

ROSS
Um, it's not that I don't appreciate
everything — 'cause, wow, do I. But there
were a couple of items that seemed a
smidge...non...wedding-ish.

STEVEN WALTHAM
(NEWS TO HIM) Such as?

IS THERE A PARTY AFTER THE SHOW?

Family Feud

"I heard Joan Collins' voice in my head as I was playing Andrea Waltham – which is a frightening thing to have happen, I can tell you."

JENNIFER SAUNDERS

*t*hink Americans don't pay attention to British TV? Well, think again. The re-runs of *Absolutely Fabulous* have been a sensation in the US ever since they first aired in 1996, and Jennifer Saunders is adored by millions of viewers who discovered her there. So it was considered quite a casting coup when she was snagged for a guest-starring role in the finale of *Friends* – although Saunders didn't exactly play hard-to-get. "I had let it be known that I wanted to do something on *Friends* the minute I heard it was coming to London," she said recently. "I wasn't shy about it, I can tell you. But then, I'm a great fan. I've seen all the shows and read all the books. And my kids, well, they love it. Really, they're the big reason I wanted to do the show."

And Tom Conti? Fuggetaboutit. Besides having a blast with the cast, he too scored major points with his brood. Both stars say that the cast is the "nicest bunch of kids" you'll ever meet; that each one personally went out of their way to make them feel a part of the ensemble during the shoot. And the writers? They were in heaven because, as one of them said admiringly, Tom Conti and Jennifer Saunders made every line ten times

"I could have said to my kids that I was going to be making a film with Robert DeNiro, Bruce Willis and Madonna and they wouldn't have blinked an eye. But when I told them that I was going to be doing a bit on Friends, they went absolutely wild. I was quite a celebrity there for a moment."

TOM CONTI

funnier. Kevin Bright fondly recalls Tom Conti's delivery of the line, "You want a piece of me, Geller?" "Of course, Tom didn't know what that line meant at first because nobody says that in England," he recalls. "So I told him it means, 'Come on, you wanna step outside and settle this?' He ended up doing it in a way that gave a nod to the fact that it was a totally unnatural thing for a British person to be saying, and it came out so hilariously funny that we found ourselves changing other lines to get the same effect." Saunders agrees: "The writers were very good with letting us do our own version of Andrea and Steven," Saunders says. "We did some improvisation at the rehearsals and then they wrote some of what we had done into the script. So, we managed to make the Walthams even more despicable."

During the summer, *Friends* brought both Conti and Saunders to Los Angeles for the first show of the fifth season – which finds them totally hysterical following the bizarre ceremony. Will they be back for more? They certainly hope so. And so does the cast. But that all depends on where Ross decides to take things with Emily and, of course, Rachel.

"I was involved in something of a scandal when I went on Rosie O'Donnell's show after I came back from England and revealed what happened with the wedding. The producers were furious with me and I can't say that I blame them. I obviously exhibited a lack of perspective, but nobody told me that the storyline was top secret. Damage control started immediately. Lisa Kudrow said in an interview that we'd shot three endings – which, of course, wasn't true. But it helped a little."

ELLIOTT GOULD

"The truth is that we had shot two endings in London – one with Ross's slip and one where we cut to Jennifer's face as the ceremony begins and then just faded out. That was an effective cliffhanger on its own. So when Elliott spilled the beans, we were able to do some damage control. I think we were more just disappointed, because we had gone to such great lengths to create a genuine cliffhanger for the end of the season, and we felt the wind had been taken out of our sails. But that's what comes from living in a world where you're so close to the show, and you want everything to be so perfect and then you realize, when it finally goes on the air, that it wasn't about the ending. It's all about the ride that takes you there."

KEVIN BRIGHT

<u>"The One With Ross's Wedding"</u> FIRST DRAFT

> ROSS
> Well, for instance...this private gym
> you built.

THIS ALL WORKED, YES?

ys

> STEVEN WALTHAM
> (JOVIAL) Oh, don't worry, Ross, you'll be
> a member.

ROSS SMILES THINLY AS WE...

CUT TO:

<u>SCENE E</u>

<u>INT. RESTAURANT - LONDON - A LITTLE LATER</u>
(NIGHT 3) (Ross, Jack Geller, Extras) ROSS COMES
BACK TO HIS DAD. HE'S LOOKING A LITTLE WORN.

> ROSS
> ("DOWN TO BUSINESS") All right. I talked to
> Waltham.

> JACK GELLER
> Yeah, what does Sir Winston
> Rip-Me-Off have to say?

LAME. LOSE?

> ROSS
> He's not gonna charge you for the gym, the
> sprinklers, and I'm making real headway on
> the new black top for the driveway.

> JACK GELLER
> Well, I should hope the hell so.

> ROSS
> <u>But</u> we're gonna need to meet him in the
> middle on some of these.

> JACK GELLER
> Meet in the middle?! If he keeps pushing
> me, my foot's gonna meet the middle of
> his ass!

> ROSS
> Dad, please. Work with me here.

CUT TO:

"The One With Ross's Wedding" FIRST DRAFT

SCENE H

INT. MONICA & RACHEL'S APT. - A BIT LATER (NIGHT 3)
(Phoebe, Rachel) PHOEBE IS IN A CHAIR. RACHEL BURSTS
INTO THE ROOM, CARRYING HER BAGS.

                    RACHEL
        (OUT OF BREATH) Hi, Pheebs.

RACHEL DROPS HER BAGS AND CROSSES TOWARD HER ROOM.

                    PHOEBE
    Oh, thank god, you changed your mind.

RACHEL EXITS INTO HER ROOM.

                    PHOEBE (CON'T.)
    (CALLING OFF) I know you love Ross, and you
    have all these feelings —

THIS SCENE HAS GOT TO MOVE FAST. WE'RE WAY OVER.

RACHEL EMERGES FROM HER BEDROOM, HOLDING HER PASSPORT.
SHE PICKS UP HER BAGS, AND HEADS FOR THE DOOR.

                    PHOEBE (CON'T.)
    Wait, where are you going?

                    RACHEL
    Bye, Pheebs.

RACHEL EXITS. PHOEBE STRUGGLES TO GET UP, BUT FAILS

                    PHOEBE
    Wait! Wait! Wait! (THEN) Ueh, why am I
    always sitting when she does that?!

how about pregnant?

                                    CUT TO:

SCENE J

INT. RESTAURANT - LONDON - A LITTLE LATER (NIGHT 3)
(Ross, Steven Waltham, Guest, Extras) ROSS AND
MR. WALTHAM ARE HUNKERED DOWN AT A TABLE, DEEP IN
NEGOTIATIONS. SHIRT SLEEVES ARE ROLLED UP, TIES ARE
LOOSENED. MR. WALTHAM IS SMOKING A CIGARETTE. ROSS
NURSES A SCOTCH.

"The One With Ross's Wedding" FIRST DRAFT

ROSS
Forget about the built-in bar-b-que.

STEVEN WALTHAM
All right, then you've got to give me the
lawn ornaments.

ROSS
I go back there with lawn ornaments, he's
going to laugh in my face.

STEVEN WALTHAM
Fine. I'll eat the lawn ornaments. But I'm
not budging on the crown moulding.

A GUEST PASSES BY.

GUEST
Lovely party.

ROSS/MR. WALTHAM
(TOTALLY PLEASANT) Thank you. Thank you so
much.

CUT TO:

SCENE K

INT. RESTAURANT - LONDON/MONICA AND RACHEL'S
APARTMENT - A LITTLE LATER (NIGHT 3/DAY 3) (Ross,
Chandler, Monica, Joey, Phoebe, Emily, Steven Waltham,
Andrea Waltham, Jack Geller, Judy Geller, Felicity,
Extras) EVERYONE HAS FINISHED EATING. CHANDLER STANDS
UP AND CLINKS HIS GLASS. EVERYONE QUIETS DOWN.

CHANDLER
Thank you. I'd like to propose a toast to
Ross and Emily. Now, of course, my big toast
is tomorrow night after the wedding. So this
is just my little toast—or melba toast, if
you will...

CHANDLER WAITS FOR THE BIG LAUGH. IT DOESN'T COME.

*let's get Mathew
to sit in with
us tonight —*

"The Walthams come back in the fifth season and they'll probably continue to get nastier and nastier - 'cause that makes them funnier and funnier.
ADAM CHASE

<u>"The One With Ross's Wedding"</u> FIRST DRAFT

                    CHANDLER (CON'T.)
Okay, uh, I've known Ross for a long time.
In fact, I knew him when he was dating his
first girlfriend. It looked like things were
really going to work out, until one day he
<u>over-inflated</u> her.
(NO RESPONSE) Oh, dear god...

MEANWHILE, MRS. WALTHAM'S MOBILE PHONE RINGS. SHE
TAKES IT OUT OF HER PURSE.

Phoebe's pregnancy will keep her grounded in New York just as Lisa Kudrow's pregnancy kept her in LA – while her fellow cast members jetted off for a glamorous jaunt to London. They had a blast, but she did pretty well too: she gave birth to a baby boy three months after filming her part of the final episode.

ANDREA WALTHAM
Hello?

INTERCUT WITH: <u>INT.
MONICA AND RACHEL'S
APT. - SAME TIME</u>

                    PHOEBE
Mrs. Waltham, hi. I need to talk to either
one of the best men, or Ross's sister,
Monica.

<u>"The One With Ross's Wedding" FIRST DRAFT</u>

ANDREA WALTHAM
Who is this?

PHOEBE
This is Phoebe Buffay. I'm one of Ross's best friends.

ANDREA WALTHAM
If you're one of Ross's best friends, why aren't you here; at the rehearsal dinner?

PHOEBE
I can't fly because I'm having my brother's babies.

What is Andrea doing here?

ANDREA WALTHAM
Am I on the radio?

PHOEBE
No. Look, I need to talk to them.

ANDREA WALTHAM
Yes, well, we're in the middle of the toasts. The one they call Chandler is speaking now.

PHOEBE
Ooo, how's it going?

> It's great fun to send up snotty English types, like we did with the Walthams, but every now and then Tom (Conti) and I would ask each other if you could get away with this kind of rabid character assassination if you were playing, say, oh I don't know, an Italian or something, in the same extremely vicious way.
> JENNIFER SAUNDERS

ANDREA WALTHAM
It's like watching the Hindenberg explode, except you wish you were on it. Now, I'm afraid I must ring off.

Does our audience know this reference?

Nah — Too young

WITH THAT, MRS. WALTHAM HANGS UP, TURNS OFF HER MOBILE PHONE, AND DROPS IT IN HER PURSE. PHOEBE IS LEFT HOLDING THE PHONE.

PHOEBE
(FRUSTRATED) The next time England calls me, I'm hanging up on it.

END INTERCUT. CHANDLER IS STILL DYING.

<u>"The One With Ross's Wedding" FIRST DRAFT</u>

CHANDLER
...And I'm sure we're all very excited to
see Ross and Emily get married tomorrow over
at Montague Hall. To think, my friend
married in Monty Hall. (AGAIN, NOTHING) Come
on, Monty Hall?! "Let's Make a Deal"?! A guy
dressed like a big carrot?! (GIVING UP,
DISGUSTED) Ah, forget it. Congratulations *Will our*
Ross and Emily. *english audience*
get this? Will
HE SITS. JOEY STANDS. *we die as*
well as
JOEY *Chandler?*
Hey. Best man number two, Joey Tribbiani. *—D.C.*
I first met Ross in this coffee
house...(GETTING A LITTLE MISTY) Yeah, the
Perk..(TRAILS OFF, NOSTALGIC) Anyway, he's
become one of my best friends. And Emily, I
hope you become one, too. I love you guys.
But not as much as I love America!

AN UNBELIEVABLY HOT BRIDESMAID, FELICITY, APPROACHES
JOEY.

FELICITY
You're going home? I was hoping I'd get to
know you better.
works every time
JOEY
(BEAT; BRIGHTLY) I don't have to go home. I
can stay as long as I want.
ON JOEY'S HAPPY SMILE...

CUT TO:

> "Ultimately I'm subscribing to the theory
> that love will happen when you don't
> look for it. I have finally stopped thinking
> that there is the one. Boy I love that
> idea, but I actually believe that there
> isn't a Miss Right. There are 12,000
> Miss Rights and it's all in the timing.
> MATTHEW PERRY

<u>"The One With Ross's Wedding"</u> FIRST DRAFT

<u>SCENE M</u>

<u>INT. RESTAURANT - LONDON - A LITTLE LATER</u> (NIGHT 3)
(Ross, Chandler, Monica, Emily, Steven Waltham, Andrea
Waltham, Jack Geller, Judy Geller, Older Guest,
Extras) THE REHEARSAL DINNER IS WRAPPING UP. PEOPLE
ARE STARTING TO LEAVE. MONICA IS COMFORTING CHANDLER.

                    MONICA
        Hey, it's not your fault. British people
        just don't have a sense of humor.

                    CHANDLER
        Yeah, that whole Monty Python drama.

SHE SQUEEZES HIS HAND, CONSOLING. HE SMILES AT HER.

                    CHANDLER (CON'T.)
        So, how are you doing?

let's get Monica drunk here

                    MONICA
        Ross is getting married and I'm happy. I'm
        not going to let anything spoil that.

AN OLDER, INTOXICATED GUEST COMES OVER.

                    OLDER GUEST
        (TO MONICA) I just want to say that Ross is
        a wonderful young man.

                    MONICA
        Oh. Thank you.

                    OLDER GUEST
        My god, you must have been a teenager when
        you had him.

MONICA'S JAW DROPS AND CHANDLER'S EYES GO WIDE.
MEANWHILE, ROSS IS ESCORTING JACK AND MR. WALTHAM OUT.

                    ROSS
        So what do you say we take the wine cellar
        and stick a pin in it for right now.

HASN'T THIS GONE TOO LONG?

<u>*"The One With Ross's Wedding"* FIRST DRAFT</u>

                  JACK GELLER
     (REASONABLE) All right, fine.

<u>JACK AND MR. WALTHAM EXIT</u>. AS <u>THEIR WIVES FOLLOW</u>,
ROSS TURNS TO HIS MOTHER.

                  ROSS
    Two cabs.

MEANWHILE, CHANDLER IS STILL WITH MONICA.

                CHANDLER
    The guy was hammered. There's no way to look
    like Ross' mother.

                MONICA
    Then why would he say it?!

                CHANDLER
    Because he's crazy! He came up to me earlier
    and thought I was (Brian Boitano.)

FUNNIEST NAME?
—D.C.

                MONICA
    (UPSET) My mom's right. I'm never going to
    get married.

                CHANDLER
    That's ridiculous. You know you're gonna
    find someone.

Leonardo diCaprio?

HE PUTS HIS ARM AROUND HER. BEAT. SHE LOOKS AT HIM.

BRITS, WON'T KNOW

                MONICA
    I totally can see (Brian Boitano.)

                      DISSOLVE TO:

                <u>SCENE P</u>

<u>INT. AIRPORT TICKET COUNTER - LATER</u> (NIGHT 3) (Rachel,
Ticket Agent, Extras) RACHEL IS ABLE TO RUN RIGHT UP
TO THE TICKET COUNTER.

                RACHEL
    Hi, I'm back. Listen, I need to get on that
    eleven o'clock.

<u>"The One With Ross's Wedding"</u> FIRST DRAFT

Sure Rachel, the ticket agent will just call the plane and tell it to come back and pick you up. And Monica doesn't like things clean.

TICKET AGENT
I'm sorry. That plane has already
pulled away from the gate.

RACHEL
Okay, you're just gonna have to call
the plane back to pick me up.

TICKET AGENT

    I can't do that.

RACHEL
(CONSPIRATORIALLY) Come on, we'll just
tell them there's a (AIR QUOTES) "funny
smell" in the cabin.

too scary
M.

<u>"The One With Ross's Wedding"</u> FIRST DRAFT

TICKET AGENT
I'm going to have to ask you to step aside,
miss. (SMILES AT NEXT CUSTOMER) Hello!

CUT TO:

*she moves to next
counter to get
away from Rachel*

<u>SCENE R</u>

<u>INT. CHANDLER & JOEY'S HOTEL ROOM – LONDON – NEXT
MORNING</u> (DAY 4) (Ross, Chandler, Monica) CHANDLER IS
IN BED. <u>ROSS BURSTS IN</u>.

ROSS
(BEAMING) I'm getting married today!

CHANDLER
Yeah, you are!

<u>ROSS EXITS</u>. MONICA POKES HER HEAD OUT
FROM UNDER THE COVERS.

MONICA
(FREAKED) Do you think he knew I
was here?

FADE OUT.

*finally!
(This makes me
so happy. The
next time we
disagree it's
yours).? M.*

<u>END OF ACT THREE</u>

79

<u>"The One With Ross's Wedding" FIRST DRAFT</u>

- ACT FOUR -

SCENE T

<u>INT. CHANDLER & JOEY'S HOTEL ROOM - LONDON - CONTINUOUS)</u> (DAY 4) (Chandler, Monica) CHANDLER AND MONICA ARE BOTH TOTALLY FREAKED OUT.

BOTH ARE IN BED, NAKED!!!

> CHANDLER
I don't know.

> *What do Mathew and Courteney think about this whole deal?*

> MONICA
I should really be —

> CHANDLER
Absolutely.

> *DON'T know about her, but he's totally into it.*

SHE STARTS TO GET OUT OF BED. THEN STOPS.

> MONICA
Could you not look?

> CHANDLER
I don't wanna look.

HE LOOKS AWAY. SHE STARTS TO GET OUT OF BED.

CUT TO:

SCENE W

<u>INT. CHANDLER & JOEY'S HOTEL ROOM - LONDON/MONICA & RACHEL'S APT. - LATER</u> (DAY 4) (Joey, Chandler (O.S.), Phoebe) THE ROOM IS EMPTY. SFX:SHOWER/SFX:PHONE RINGING/SFX: JOEY ENTERS.

> JOEY
Phone!

> CHANDLER (O.S.)
Shower!

> JOEY
Okay! Hey, hooked up with a girl last night.

> CHANDLER (O.S.)
I didn't! Stayed here! Went right to sleep! No girl!

<u>"The One With Ross's Wedding"</u> FIRST DRAFT

JOEY PICKS UP THE PHONE.

        JOEY
 Hello?

<u>INTERCUT WITH: INT. MONICA & RACHEL'S APT.</u> - SAME
TIME. PHOEBE IS ON THE PHONE.

       PHOEBE
 Where the hell have you been?!

        JOEY
 Hey. I spent the night out. I met this cute
 bridesmaid. Oh, man, she is so –

Although well along into her own pregnancy at the time of shooting, Lisa Kudrow was wrapped in extra padding by costume designer Debra McGuire in order to make her appear to be carrying triplets.

<u>"The One With Ross's Wedding" FIRST DRAFT</u>

PHOEBE
We have an emergency! Rachel is coming to
London!

JOEY
Oh, great!

PHOEBE
No, not great! She's coming to tell Ross she
loves him.

JOEY
But he loves Emily.

PHOEBE
You have to do something!

JOEY
Like what?

PHOEBE
I don't know. Stop her. Don't let her
wreck the wedding.

JOEY
Okay.

PHOEBE
(INTENSE) So, okay. I've done my part.
It's your responsibility now. The burden
is off me. Right?

JOEY
Right.

PHOEBE
All right. (THEN, CHATTY) So, tell me about
this girl.

CUT TO:

London Baby!

*not so fast—
we've still got to
rewrite this
script
about a
billion times!*

> "Playing dumb blondes was the easiest way
> to get experience. I didn't dare judge it.
> There was no 'What does this mean for
> society?' But along the way, I saw
> advantages to playing dumb in real life too.
> People don't expect much. You're in the
> perfect position for ambush."
>
> LISA KUDROW

<u>"The One With Ross's Wedding"</u> FIRST DRAFT

<u>SCENE X</u>

<u>INT. AIRPLANE - SAME TIME</u> (DAY 4) (Rachel, Gentleman, Extras) RACHEL IS IN HER SEAT, WAITING TO TAKE OFF. SHE ANXIOUSLY TAPS AND DRUMS. SHE LEAFS THROUGH A MAGAZINE, THEN TOSSES IT ASIDE. SHE SIGHS AND TAPS SOME MORE. THE DROLL, SOPHISTICATED MAN IN THE NEXT SEAT TURNS TO HER.

                    GENTLEMAN
        If you're planning on doing that for the
        entire flight, please tell me now, so I can
        take a sedative. Or, perhaps slip you one.

                    RACHEL
        (STOPPING) I'm sorry. I'm sorry. (BEAT,
        THEN) It's just, I'm kinda excited. I'm
        going to London to tell this guy I love him.

HE LOOKS AT HER FOR A BEAT, THEN TURNS AWAY AND PUTS ON HIS HEADPHONES. BEAT. RACHEL TURNS TO THE PERSON IN THE OTHER SEAT.

                                        CUT TO:
                <u>SCENE Y</u>

<u>INT. CHANDLER & JOEY'S HOTEL ROOM - A LITTLE LATER</u> (DAY 4) JOEY HANGS UP THE PHONE. <u>CHANDLER EMERGES FROM THE BATHROOM</u> IN A BATHROBE.

                    JOEY
        Have you seen Monica?

MOVE THIS TO THE WEDDING?

                    CHANDLER
        (PANIC) I'm not seeing Monica.

                    JOEY
        We've got to find her. Phoebe just called.
        Rachel's coming to tell Ross she loves him.

                    CHANDLER
        That's not good.

                    JOEY
        I know.

Helen Baxendale

*h*elen Baxendale was on a publicity tour in the US for her television show, *An Unsuitable Job for a Woman*, when she got word that she had been chosen for a starring role in *Friends*. She went right into the part of Emily, Ross's new love interest, without missing a beat – or going back to London. She had impressed the *Friends* producers during secret auditions held in London at the start of the year, but gave up hope on the job once stories started appearing saying that Patsy Kensit had gotten the part. Kensit did indeed go to LA to work with the cast, but somehow things just didn't click. "The thing that's toughest for a new person coming into *Friends* is that the six of them are such a tight ensemble," says producer Kevin Bright. "They have a shorthand that is really intimidating for a guest actor to walk into. I think Patsy hadn't ever done a sitcom like *Friends* before and it all became kind of overwhelming." Kensit's departure opened the door for Helen Baxendale – who, in everyone's mind, turned out to be the perfect choice for the role. She was crisply exotic, thin and sophisticated, with angular features. And instead of being warm and neurotic, she was tart and edgy. "What we wanted from our Emily was that she feel very different from our three women," continues Bright. "Helen was someone you could believe was right for Ross. Yes, she was a little bit stronger than the other women he'd been with, but I think he liked her that way."

"Helen Baxendale is doing great. She won people over the minute she made her first entrance on the show. It's like, wow, something a little different."
MATTHEW PERRY

"I felt sorry for her (Helen Baxendale) at first. She arrived on Thursday, ready to start filming on Friday and she was sitting with us, and Jennifer and I are so close and we were talking about the most personal things. I think she was a little shocked at how open we are."

COURTENEY COX

"Look out Helen, there's one of the paparazzi over there shooting our photo."

"All right then, I'll give him my good side ..."

"The One With Ross's Wedding" FIRST DRAFT

                    CHANDLER
(ON THE EDGE) Friends should not get
involved with other friends.

                    JOEY
Are you okay?

                    CHANDLER
(QUICKLY COVERING) I'm, uh, homesick.

                    JOEY
You know what you gotta do? You gotta hook
up with a bridesmaid. Oh, wait, the only
other bridesmaid is Monica.

CHANDLER STARTS TO LAUGH AND HYPERVENTILATE AT THE
SAME TIME.

                                    CUT TO:

                    SCENE Z

INT. AIRPLANE - SAME TIME (DAY 4) (Rachel, Gentleman,
Extras) RACHEL IS STILL TALKING TO THE OTHER
PASSENGER, DEEP INTO HER STORY.

                    RACHEL
And I realized all this crazy stuff I've
been doing — Joshua, and re-upholstering the
couch — it's all just a way of —

THE GENTLEMAN TAKES OFF HIS HEADPHONES

— we cut this, remember?

                    GENTLEMAN
If I may interrupt. I'm afraid I have to
agree with your friend Pheebs, this is a
terrible plan.

                    RACHEL
But he's got to know how I feel.

                    GENTLEMAN
Why? He loves this Emily.
No good can come of this.

> "When somebody follows you twenty blocks to the pharmacy. where they watch you buy toilet paper, you know your life has changed.
> JENNIFER ANISTON
> on the pressures of fame

<u>"The One With Ross's Wedding"</u> FIRST DRAFT

                    RACHEL
    Well, I think you're wrong.

THE GENTLEMAN PUTS HIS HEADPHONES BACK ON AND RETURNS
TO IGNORING HER.

                                        DISSOLVE TO:

                    <u>SCENE ZZ</u>

<u>INT. MONTAGUE HALL/ANTEROOM - LONDON - THAT NIGHT</u>
(NIGHT 4) (Monica, Ross, Joey, Chandler, Rachel,
Emily, Jack Geller, Judy Geller, Steven Waltham,
Andrea Waltham, Felicity, Extras) THE HALL HAS BEEN
TRANSFORMED. FLOWERS AND CANDLES ABOUND. TWINKLY
LIGHTS HAVE BEEN STRUNG FROM WALL TO WALL. IT'S
ABOUT AN HOUR BEFORE THE WEDDING. MONICA, EMILY,
AND JUDY ARE MARVELING AT THE ROOM.

                    JUDY GELLER
    It's like a fairyland.

                    EMILY
    It's really beautiful, isn't it?

JOEY COMES OVER.

                    JOEY
    Psst. Monica.
HE PULLS HER ASIDE. <u>JUDY AND EMILY MOVE OFF</u>.

                    JOEY (CON'T.)
    We should really start watching out for
    Rachel. How about if I cover the front door,
    and you watch that big hole at the back of
    the building.

                    MONICA
    You got it.

                    JOEY
    And I've got Chandler guarding Ross.

<u>MONICA MOVES OFF</u>.

                                        RESET TO:

87

<u>"The One With Ross's Wedding"</u> FIRST DRAFT

<u>INT. ANTEROOM - CONTINUOUS</u>. ROSS AND CHANDLER ARE CHECKING THEMSELVES OUT. ROSS IS A LITTLE KEYED UP.

                    CHANDLER
        You look great, man.

                    ROSS
        Thanks. You can't tell I'm sweating?

                    CHANDLER
        Not at all.

                    ROSS
        What if it gets as bad as last time?

                    CHANDLER
        I put a half a diaper in each pocket.
        Just slip 'em in your pits.

                    ROSS
        (PATTING POCKETS) Thanks, man.

Hut!? WHAT KIND OF DIAPER? BABY OR DEPENDS?

                                    RESET TO:

<u>INT. MONTAGUE HALL - CONTINUOUS</u>. JOEY'S GUARDING THE DOOR. <u>FELICITY ENTERS</u>.

                    FELICITY
        Hi, Joey.

HOW ABOOT ROSS PRACTICING HIS "I-DO'S"

                    JOEY
        Hey, Felicity.

                    FELICITY
        I thought about you all day.

                    JOEY
        Yeah?

                    FELICITY
        (INTIMATE) Talk New York to me again.

                    JOEY
        Fuggetaboutit.

let's add nis: "How you doin'?"

SHE LIKES THIS.

"The One With Ross's Wedding" FIRST DRAFT

FELICITY

Ooo...

SHE SQUEALS AND KISSES HIM. THEY DUCK BEHIND A
PILLAR.

RESET TO:

INT. ANTEROOM - CONTINUOUS. ROSS IS TESTING HIS
ARMPITS.

ROSS
(PLEASED) Can't even feel them.

CHANDLER
I'll get you some more.

NAH

HE EXITS. BEAT.RESET TO:
INT. MONTAGUE HALL - CONTINUOUS. JACK AND MR. WALTHAM
ARE FACING OFF. THE WIVES ARE NEARBY.

JACK GELLER
Not only am I not paying for that wine
cellar, now I'm not paying for the crown
moulding!

Emily might have had
an inkling of problems
to come if she'd seen
Rachel come rushing
into Montgomery Hall
– as she did in this
draft. But she will
remain blissfully
unaware that anything
is amiss until it is
time for Ross to
recite his vows.

<u>"The One With Ross's Wedding"</u> FIRST DRAFT

MR. WALTHAM GASPS. <u>EMILY RUNS OUT</u>.

                    EMILY
What's going on?

                    ROSS
Don't worry, I've got everything under
control.

                STEVEN WALTHAM
You want a piece of me, Geller? You want a
piece of me?!

                    EMILY
(TO ROSS) You know, it doesn't seem like
you do.

                    ROSS
All right! That's it! Parents, back away!
This is our wedding day!

                  PARENTS
(COWED) Absolutely. You're right.
Very sorry.

<u>THE PARENTS EXIT</u>.

                    EMILY
What was that about?

                    ROSS
(COMING CLEAN) Okay, there was a discrepancy
over — God, you look beautiful.

MEANWHILE, OVER BY THE DOOR, JOEY IS STILL MAKING OUT
WITH FELICITY. THEY ARE UNAWARE AS <u>RACHEL ENTERS</u>. SHE
RUSHES PAST THEM. SHE COMES INTO THE MAIN HALL AND
SEES ROSS AND EMILY. THEY ARE VERY CLOSE AND HE IS
HOLDING HER HANDS. THEY KISS. RACHEL TAKES THIS IN.
AFTER A MOMENT, ROSS NOTICES RACHEL.
RACHEL TAKES A BEAT. THEN:

[Handwritten note:] ARE THEY ALL STANDING TOGETHER HERE?

[Handwritten note:] WE NEED A REAL THREAT... HOW ABOUT "NO GRANDCHILDREN!

<u>"The One With Ross's Wedding"</u> FIRST DRAFT

> " I want Ross to find another relationship away from Rachel. But it would be nice to come back to the relationship with her and then eventually marry. Will it happen? The writers can do almost anything they want."
> DAVID SCHWIMMER

Rachel rushes into Montgomery Hall and sees Ross and Emily locked in a happy embrace.

ROSS
Rach? I can't believe it! What are you doing here?!

RACHEL
I just wanted to be here to say congratulations.

ROSS
I'm so glad.

HE HUGS HER. EMILY LOOKS ON, PLEASED.

would she really be pleased?

DISSOLVE TO:

<u>SCENE YY</u>

<u>INT. MONTAGUE HALL - LONDON/MONICA & RACHEL'S APT. -
NIGHT/DAY</u> (NIGHT 4/DAY 4) (Monica, Phoebe, Rachel,
Ross, Chandler, Joey, Emily, Andrea Waltham, Steven
Waltham, Jack Geller, Judy Geller, Judge, Felicity,
Extras) THE CEREMONY IS BEGINNING. MUSIC IS PLAYING.
THE LAST FEW PEOPLE FIND THEIR SEATS. <u>ROSS ENTERS
FROM THE SIDE</u> AND CROSSES TO THE PODIUM. THE
PROCESSIONAL BEGINS. <u>JOEY ENTERS</u> FROM THE BACK <u>WITH
THE MAID OF HONOR</u> AND STARTS WALKING DOWN THE AISLE.

"The One With Ross's Wedding" FIRST DRAFT

MRS. WALTHAM'S MOBILE PHONE RINGS. SHE ANSWERS IT.

              ANDREA WALTHAM
  Hello?

INTERCUT WITH: INT. MONICA & RACHEL'S APT. -
CONTINUOUS

                PHOEBE
  Hi, it's Phoebe again.

              ANDREA WALTHAM
  Why do you keep calling me?

                PHOEBE
  Can I please, please, please talk to one
  of the best men?

JOEY, WALKING DOWN THE AISLE, PASSES BY.

              ANDREA WALTHAM
  Joseph, there's a girl on the phone for you.

                JOEY
  (SUPER-CASUAL) Oh, great. (INTO PHONE)
  Hello?

HE CONTINUES IN THE PROCESSIONAL.

                PHOEBE
  Joey, it's Phoebe. What happened? Did you
  stop Rachel?

                JOEY
  No, but it's okay. She just came and gave
  him a hug. That's it.

                PHOEBE
  Nothing got ruined? That's so great. (THEN)
  What's going on now?

                JOEY
  Okay, I'm walking down the aisle. I better
  go.

[Handwritten note:] STILL WALKING DOWN THE AISLE

[Handwritten note:] Andrea is pissed here, right?

<u>"The One With Ross's Wedding"</u> FIRST DRAFT

                        PHOEBE
        Wait. Hold up the phone, so I can listen.

HE HOLDS UP THE MOBILE PHONE SO SHE CAN HEAR.
MEANWHILE, MONICA AND CHANDLER ARE COMING DOWN THE
AISLE TOGETHER. THEY ARE JUST AS AWKWARD AS BEFORE.

                        CHANDLER
        What happened last night was...

                                    Money, Baby!
                                    $

                        MONICA
        Stupid.

                        CHANDLER
        What were we thinking? (BEAT) But I'm coming
        to your room tonight, right?

                        MONICA
        Oh, yeah. Definitely.

THE MUSIC SHIFTS TO THE WEDDING MARCH, AS MR. WALTHAM
WALKS EMILY DOWN THE AISLE. ROSS SMILES AT HER. SHE
SMILES BACK. THEY REACH THE FRONT AND STOP. AS ROSS
APPROACHES, THEM, JACK LOOKS UP AT MR. WALTHAM AND
MUTTERS:

                        JACK GELLER
        Not paying for it.

> 66 There was a big debate over whether we
> should even try to pull this whole [London
> wedding] thing off: I mean, do we wanna
> kill ourselves shooting all the setup that
> we needed – to get Emily to New York
> and get her together with Ross in the first
> place. It was obviously going to be a
> nightmare. But then we all said 'Yeah, sure,
> let's give it a shot.' And when Helen came
> in, everybody was really glad that we did,
> 'cause she was great and absolutely right
> for the role, perfect.
>   ADAM CHASE 99

<u>"The One With Ross's Wedding"</u> FIRST DRAFT

                    STEVEN WALTHAM
         You're paying for it.

MR. WALTHAM GIVES JACK ONE FINAL DARK LOOK AND THEN
SITS DOWN NEXT TO HIS WIFE. ROSS AND EMILY TURN TO
THE JUDGE WHO'S OFFICIATING.

                        JUDGE
         Friends, family, we are gathered here to
         celebrate the joyous union of Ross and
         Emily. Emily, repeat after me:
         I, Emily...

                        EMILY
         I, Emily...

                        JUDGE

         Take thee, Ross...

Is he or she a minister

                        EMILY
         Take thee, Ross...

No, this is non-denominational, remember?

                        JUDGE
         As my lawfully wedded husband,
         in sickness and in health,
         until death parts us...

WHY? SO WE CAN OFFEND EVERYBODY?

                        EMILY
         As my lawfully wedded husband,
         in sickness and in health,
         until death parts us...

WE SEE RACHEL TAKE THIS IN.
THE JUDGE TURNS TO ROSS.

                        JUDGE
         Ross, repeat after me: I, Ross...

                        ROSS
         I, Ross...

                        JUDGE
         Take thee, Emily...

<u>"The One With Ross's Wedding"</u> FIRST DRAFT

> ROSS
> Take thee, Rachel — Emily —

ROSS CAN'T BELIEVE WHAT JUST HAPPENED. HE SHUTS HIS
EYES. EMILY IS SHOCKED. WE SEE MONICA, JOEY AND
CHANDLER'S STUNNED REACTIONS. WE SEE RACHEL'S
ASTONISHED EXPRESSION. WE SEE THE WALTHAMS,
THE GELLERS. WE SEE PHOEBE GASP AT HOME.
FINALLY:

> JUDGE
> (TO EMILY, TENTATIVE) Uh, shall I go on?

ARE WE GOING TO LET THE BRITISH STUDIO AUDIENCE SEE THIS?

?

AS THIS QUESTION HANGS IN THE AIR...

<u>END OF SHOW</u>

FADE OUT. *No!*

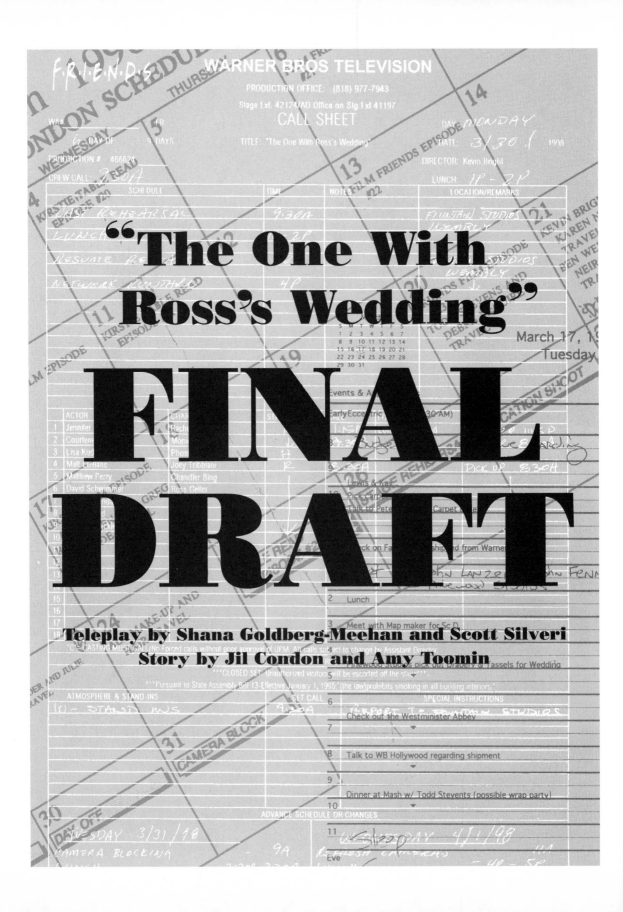

"The One With Ross's Wedding"

FINAL DRAFT

Teleplay by Shana Goldberg-Meehan and Scott Silveri

Story by Jil Condon and Amy Toomin

TEASER

SCENE A
FADE IN: <u>INT. CHANDLER & JOEY'S APT./MONICA & RACHEL'S APT. - DAY</u> (DAY 1) (Chandler, Joey, Phoebe, Rachel, Monica, Ross) THE DOORS TO BOTH APARTMENTS ARE OPEN. JOEY AND CHANDLER ARE FINISHING PACKING THEIR LUGGAGE. <u>MONICA STICKS HER HEAD IN</u>.

MONICA
You guys, hurry up! The flight leaves in four hours. It may take us some time to find a taxi. There could be traffic. The plane could leave early. When we get to London, there could be a line at Customs. Come on!

<u>SHE GOES</u> BACK TO HER APARTMENT.

CHANDLER
It's a six-hour trip to London. That's a lot of Monica.

RESET TO: <u>INT. MONICA & RACHEL'S APT. - CONTINUOUS</u>. PHOEBE'S LYING ON THE COUCH. RACHEL'S HANGING OUT, MONICA'S BAGS ARE PACKED, AND SHE'S GOING THROUGH HER CARRY-ON.

MONICA
Passport. Check. Camera. Check. Travelers' checks. Check.

RACHEL
Who are you saying check to?

MONICA
Myself. For remembering to pack the thing. You know, you do a good thing, you get a check. (THEN) My mom does it. I never realized it was weird.

PHOEBE
My mom used to put her head in the oven. Well, she only did it the one time, but it was pretty weird.

<u>ROSS ENTERS</u> WITH LUGGAGE. AD-LIB HELLOS.

ROSS
(TO MONICA) You almost ready?

MONICA
Yep. You got the tickets?

ROSS
(SHOWS THEM) Got 'em right here. Check.

RESET TO: <u>INT. CHANDLER & JOEY'S APT. - CONTINUOUS</u>. THEY PICK UP THEIR BAGS AND HEAD FOR THE DOOR.

> JOEY
>
> All London, baby! Here we go!

> CHANDLER
>
> You got your passport?

> JOEY
>
> It's in the third drawer on my dresser. You don't want to lose that. (THEN) Oh.

AS <u>JOEY EXITS</u> TO HIS ROOM, WE...

FADE OUT.

Joey's "London Baby!" riff has grown bigger in this draft, but his constant bickering with Chandler and his trip to McDonald's have been trimmed in order to make room for his rendezvous with a certain royal who goes by the name of Fergie.

MAKING FRIENDS IN THE U.K.
FINAL DRAFT

<u>ACT ONE</u>

<u>SCENE B</u>

FADE IN: <u>INT. MONICA & RACHEL'S APT. - MOMENTS LATER</u> (DAY 1) (Monica, Rachel, Phoebe, Ross, Chandler, Joey) MONICA, PHOEBE, RACHEL AND ROSS ARE THERE. MONICA IS GOING OVER SOME STUFF WITH PHOEBE.

MONICA

Okay, if you need the vacuum, it's in my closet on the left. The garbage bags are next to the refrigerator.

PHOEBE

Rachel's gonna be here, too. Can't I just ask her this stuff?

MONICA

(CRACKING UP) Yeah, okay. Give that a try.

<u>JOEY AND CHANDLER ENTER</u>. AD-LIB HELLOS.

ROSS

All right. We're all here.

THE OTHERS

Whoo-hoo. Yeah. All right.

JOEY

London, baby!

> We all know how lucky we are to have a great job. We enjoy each other's company, and that's all I need to keep me happy.
> DAVID SCHWIMMER

CHANDLER

Oh, that's not gonna get annoying.

JOEY

(IN CHANDLER'S FACE) London, baby!

CHANDLER

Oh, I guess I was wrong.

ROSS

We're all here. I guess we should get going.

PHOEBE

Aww. I'd come over there and hug you, and wish you good luck with your wedding, but it's too hard for me to get up.

ROSS

(STARTS TOWARDS PHOEBE) Oh, then I'll come hug —

PHOEBE

Yeah, and bring me that newspaper.

HE TURNS BACK, TAKES THE NEWSPAPER OFF THE KITCHEN TABLE, AND BRINGS IT TO PHOEBE. AS THEY HUG...

> PHOEBE (CON'T.)
> Have a great wedding. (THEN) And Chandler, I want to hug you, too.

CHANDLER, WHO'S ABOUT TWO STEPS AWAY, STARTS FOR PHOEBE.

> PHOEBE (CON'T.)
> And you might as well bring me my book. It's on the counter in your apartment.

> CHANDLER
> (NOT PLEASED) You got it.

HE EXITS.

> ROSS
> (TO RACHEL) So...we're off.

> RACHEL
> (HUGS HIM) Have fun.

> ROSS
> I can't believe you're not going to be there.

> RACHEL
> I know.

> ROSS
> So, why don't you come?

> RACHEL
> What?

> ROSS
> Come to London. Please. It would mean so much to me.

> RACHEL
> I gotta work. I'm sorry.

> ROSS
> You can't take a couple of days off?

> RACHEL
> Because I can't Ross. I told you.

Poor Ross. His whole life is just one jaw-dropping double-take after another

ROSS

This is my <u>wedding</u>.

MONICA

(PICKING UP HER BAGS) All right. Now we're actually late. Let's go. Let's go. Let's go.

ROSS LOOKS TO RACHEL. SHE'S UNYIELDING. THEN...

ROSS

Fine. You can watch it on video when we get back.

AS HE CROSSES AWAY, <u>CHANDLER ENTERS</u>, WITH PHOEBE'S BOOK.

PHOEBE

Thank you.

Follow Chandler's goodbye to Phoebe in the script and watch Matthew Perry transform his lines into "Chandler-speak".

HE STANDS BY WAITING FOR HIS HUG

PHOEBE (CON'T.)

(NOTICING) Oh, right.

PHOEBE GIVES HIM A PAT ON THE HEAD AND OPENS UP HER BOOK.

ROSS

Well, let's go.

                    JOEY
        London, baby!

CHANDLER, JOEY, ROSS AND MONICA ALL PICK UP THEIR BAGS, AD-LIB GOODBYES TO
PHOEBE AND RACHEL. THEY EXIT. RACHEL LOOKS AFTER ROSS, SADLY.

                    PHOEBE
        Do you need a hug? (OFF RACHEL'S LOOK) You don't have to bring me
        anything.

                                            DISSOLVE TO:

                    SCENE C

EXT. HOTEL - LONDON - THE NEXT DAY (DAY 2) (Joey, Chandler, Extras) JOEY AND CHANDLER
EXIT THE HOTEL. JOEY IS CARRYING A GUIDE BOOK IN ONE HAND, AND A VIDEO CAMERA IN
THE OTHER. HE HAS SEVERAL MAPS AND BROCHURES STICKING OUT OF HIS POCKET. HE'S
FILMING CHANDLER. CHANDLER IS TRYING TO MOVE AWAY FROM HIM.

                    JOEY
        Come on, do something.

                    CHANDLER
        I am. I'm ignoring you.

                    JOEY
        All right, you suck. I'm going to be the on-camera guy.

HE HANDS CHANDLER THE CAMERA.

                    JOEY (CON'T.)
        All right, first stop…Westminster Abbey.

HE WHIPS OUT A GIANT POP-UP MAP OF LONDON.

                    CHANDLER
        (HORRIFIED) What is that?

                    JOEY
        London, baby.

CHANDLER LOOKS AROUND, SELF-CONSCIOUS.

> " It's funny playing a bad
> actor on the show. It
> cracks me up. It can be
> hard to differentiate
> between the way I
> approach a scene as Matt
> and the way Joey would
> approach a scene. "
> MATT LE BLANC

"Matt wanted a photo with us to prove to his family that he really knows the writers," claims Adam Chase (far right) who, along with Michael Borkow, Michael Curtis and Greg Malins, make Matt's day.

JOEY

All right, we are here... (LOOKING AROUND) Wait. (RE: MAP) I think we're actually <u>here</u>. (THEN) I know... (PUTTING MAP ON GROUND) I'm gonna have to go into the map.

JOEY STEPS INTO THE MAP TO GET HIS BEARINGS.

CHANDLER

All right. If you see a little version of me in there, kill it!

JOEY

All right. Here we go.

JOEY CAREFULLY STEPS OUT OF THE MAP AND HOLDS IT IN FRONT OF HIMSELF LIKE A TRAY. HE STARTS TO WALK.

CHANDLER

(MORTIFIED) Are we gonna have to walk like this the entire time?

JOEY

(CONCENTRATING) Shh! (THEN) Oh, man. You made me lose it.

AS JOEY PLACES THE MAP BACK ON THE GROUND AND STEPS BACK INTO IT, WE...

CUT TO:

> "The walk-in map went through three different versions until we came up with the one that Kevin fell in love with. With something like that, you don't want it to be too silly, too over the top."
> GREG GRANDE

> "It had been raining literally right up until the second we were ready to shoot Joey and Chandler's first outdoor sequence. We used a crane with a remote control camera to follow the guys out of the hotel and on to the street in one fluid shot. Fortunately, we were able to shoot this scene before the press announced where we would be shooting, so we had a relatively easy time capturing a tricky camera move without having to worry about catching fans in the shot. Later in the day, a radio station announced our locations, and we were besieged with photographers and fans which, by the way, was great. It was like having a studio audience on location."
>
> KEVIN BRIGHT

SCENE D

EXT. LONDON STREET A - A BIT LATER (DAY 2) (Monica, Ross, Emily, Construction Workers, Extras) MONICA, ROSS AND EMILY ARE WALKING DOWN THE STREET. EMILY IS IN A FAIRLY MANIC STATE.

EMILY

(ON A RANT) That was all before ten o'clock. And then the caterer rang to say it's going to be chicken Kiev instead of chicken tarragon. And then the florist phoned to say there aren't any tulips. And the cellist has carpal-tunnel syndrome.

ROSS

(STOPPING) Whoa. Emily. Honey. Okay?

HE MAKES THE TIME-OUT SIGN.

EMILY

(OFFENDED) Well, up yours, too!

ROSS

No. That's time-out. Relax. Everything's going to be great.

MONICA

(WITH DISTASTE) Chicken Kiev?

ROSS

(POINTEDLY) Mmm-hmm. Doesn't that sound delicious at the last minute?

Monica sings the praises of poached salmon to Emily and Ross, but they're committed to the chicken Kiev.

MONICA

I know. But something like salmon would be more elegant, and you wouldn't have to worry about salmonella. (OFF ROSS' INTENSE GLARE, RETREATING) So I can't wait to see where you're getting married.

THEY START TO WALK AGAIN.

ROSS

It's so beautiful. Emily's parents got married there.

EMILY

I still can't believe they're going to tear it down. It really is the most lovely building you'll ever see. It's right over—

THEY TURN THE CORNER AND SEE THAT THE HALL HAS BEEN PARTIALLY DEMOLISHED. ALL THAT REMAINS ARE MOST OF THE FOUR WALLS, AND A PILE OF RUBBLE ON THE GROUND. THERE ARE CONSTRUCTION WORKERS THERE. ROSS AND EMILY ARE STUNNED.

EMILY

Oh my God…

MONICA

It's nice.

CUT TO:

SCENE DX

INT. MONTGOMERY HALL - LONDON - MOMENTS LATER (DAY 2) (Ross, Monica, Emily) THE HALL IS PARTIALLY DEMOLISHED. THERE IS RUBBLE AND BRICKS EVERYWHERE. ROSS AND EMILY ENTER AND LOOK AROUND.

EMILY

(UPSET) Oh, my god! How can this happen?! What are we going to do?!

ROSS

(COMFORTING) It's all right. It's going to be all right.

EMILY

(FREAKED) How is it all right?

ROSS

(BEAT) Uh-huh, I see that.

MONICA ENTERS.

MONICA

Okay, I talked to the guy with the shovel, and found out what happened.

Courteney Cox, Helen Baxendale and David Schwimmer had only seconds to nail this scene in which they discover the demolished Montgomery Hall, because director Kevin Bright wanted to capture a ferry that happened to be passing on the river behind them in the scene.
ABOVE: the threesome strolls, then runs, towards the scene of the disaster – all with a platoon of fans and photographers packed into barricades behind them. Afterwards, they gather for a promised photo opportunity.

ROSS/EMILY

What? What?

MONICA

They tore it down a few days early.

CUT TO:

SCENE E

EXT. WESTMINSTER ABBEY - LONDON - LATER (DAY 2) (Chandler, Joey, Extras) CHANDLER AND
JOEY ARE ADMIRING THE ABBEY.

JOEY

All right! Westminster Abbey. Hands down, best abbey I've ever seen.
(POINTING CAMERA AT CHANDLER) What'd you think of the Abbey,
Chandler?

CHANDLER

It's great. You know, they're thinking of changing the name of this place.

JOEY

Oh really…to what?

CHANDLER

To put the camera away!

" Chandler is a slightly
exaggerated form of me –
a little more neurotic and
pathetic. I have to say,
though, that I'm enjoying
the fact that he's growing
up a little bit. "
MATTHEW PERRY

JOEY

Man, you are Westminster <u>C</u>rabby.

CUT TO:

SCENE H

<u>INT. DRESS SHOP - LONDON - LATER</u> (DAY 2) MONICA'S TRYING ON HER BRIDESMAID DRESS. EMILY'S WITH HER, AND STRESSED OUT. THE SALESLADY PINS THE DRESS.

SCENE DELETED

DISSOLVE TO:

SCENE K

<u>INT. MONICA & RACHEL'S APT. - LATER</u> (DAY 2) (Rachel, Phoebe) PHOEBE'S LYING ON THE COUCH, READING HER BOOK. AFTER A MOMENT SHE STARTS TO SQUIRM AROUND A BIT. <u>RACHEL ENTERS.</u>

RACHEL

(NOTICES PHOEBE) Hey, don't get up. I'll do it. What do you need?

PHOEBE

Nothing.

RACHEL

Come on, Pheebs. I'm here to take care of you.

PHOEBE

Okay. I have a wedgie.

RACHEL

(BEAT) That's all you.

PHOEBE

So, what do you want to do for lunch?

RACHEL

(BUMMED) I don't know. I guess we have to eat.

PHOEBE

Well, <u>I</u> do. What's the matter?

RACHEL

I'm just bummed about the way I left things with Ross. I wish I hadn't lied to him about having to work. He seemed so mad at me.

Bright Kauffman Crane
productions

1. Read script with London cast
2. Re-write script
3. Fight jet lag
4. Make reservations for Jeffrey's birthday
5. First run-thru
6. Re-write script
7. Dinner with Richard Branson (get his "take" on the character)
8. Get tickets to "Art"
9. Final run-thru
10. Re-write script
11. Read new writers for "Veronica's Closet"
12. Camera block show
13. Re-write script
14. Give notes on Ira's latest draft of "Jesse"
15 Write scenes for first episode for next season
16. Drink too much beer at the last show

DAVID CRANE

PHOEBE

Don't be so hard on yourself. I mean, if someone I was still in love with was getting married —

RACHEL

Someone you were still in <u>love</u> with?

PHOEBE

Yeah.

RACHEL

(DEFENSIVE) I'm not in love with Ross.

PHOEBE

(BACKING OFF) Oh. No. Good. Me neither.

RACHEL

I'm not going to Ross's wedding because he's my ex-boyfriend and that would be really uncomfortable. Not because I'm still in love with him. I like Ross as much as the next guy. I mean, clearly I have feelings for him. But feelings don't mean love. Do I have <u>loving</u> feelings for Ross? (THINKS) Yeah, I mean I have continuing feelings of love, but that doesn't mean I'm still <u>in</u> love with him. I have sexual feelings for him, but I <u>do</u> love him.

PHOEBE WATCHES RACHEL WARILY, AS RACHEL HEARS WHAT SHE JUST SAID.THEN...

RACHEL (CON'T.)

(EXPLODING) Oh my god! Why didn't you tell me?!?

PHOEBE

Well, we just thought —

RACHEL

We??

PHOEBE

Oh, yeah. We all know. We talk about it all the time.

> I don't want [the six characters] to be living together when we're 70. Eventually we're going to have to evolve, move on.
> JENNIFER ANISTON

RACHEL

You <u>all</u> know?! Does Ross know?!

PHOEBE

Oh, no, Ross doesn't know anything.

RACHEL

I can't believe you didn't tell me!

PHOEBE

We thought you knew. It was so obvious. It'd be like telling Monica, Hey, you like things clean.

CUT TO:

SCENE M

<u>EXT. TOWER OF LONDON - LONDON - LATER</u> (DAY 2) (Chandler, Joey, Vendor, Extras)
CHANDLER AND JOEY APPROACH A SOUVENIR STAND. THE WHEELER-DEALER VENDOR
COMES UP.

> VENDOR
> So, what are you fine gentlemen in the market for? Scarves? Souvenir
> postcards?

> JOEY
> Hey, check this out.

HE TRIES ON A BIG, FLOPPY, UNION JACK HAT.

> JOEY (CON'T.)
> (ADMIRING HIMSELF) Ooh. That's the stuff.

> JOEY
> (TO CHANDLER, RE: THE HAT) Seriously, what do you think?

> CHANDLER
> Well, now I won't have to buy that I'm With Stupid t-shirt anymore.

> JOEY
> I like it.

JOEY STARTS TO PAY THE VENDOR.

> CHANDLER
> You're not really gonna <u>buy</u> that. Look, you've already embarrassed me
> enough for one day.

> JOEY
> I embarrass you?

> CHANDLER
> How can I answer that when I'm pretending I don't know you?

> VENDOR
> (TO JOEY) He's just jealous. You'll fit right in in that. All Londoners wear
> them.

> CHANDLER
> Then how come no one here anywhere is wearing one?

> VENDOR
> (IT'S OBVIOUS) They're all tourists.

Richard Branson

*V*irgin entrepreneur Richard Branson was first buzzed about doing a cameo role on *Friends* during Kevin Bright's preliminary visit to London for a reality check of the problems involved in bringing his whole brood in for the season finale. When asked to comment at the time, a spokesman for Branson said, "He has been approached and he's considering it. Richard's children love *Friends* – as does he – so naturally he's going to talk to them."

After agreeing to do the part, Branson's only request was that it be kept short. And so it was with the creation of a character named "Tricky Dick", an oily street peddler, for the world-famous wheeler-dealer. But although his whole part consisted of a very few lines, he had a little trouble nailing it and ended up requiring many, many takes. But then, Branson probably had other things on his mind. "He had just come from a meeting with literally, like, the Prime Minister of Israel," says Adam Chase, "and he didn't have time to completely memorize the script." Greg Malins chimes in, "Apparently, at the meeting, he had asked the Prime Minister of Israel to run lines with him, but he didn't have time to do it." But if Branson had any problems with his delivery, you'd never know it from the finished take. He's funny and sharp and appropriately pushy, and he sets up Joey and Chandler for their bits like a pro. No doubt he'll be getting more acting offers as a result. Hey, it's safer than hot-air ballooning around the world.

> "I've definitely gone up in my children's estimation. I think now that I've appeared on *Friends* I've finally got their respect."
>
> RICHARD BRANSON

Matthew Perry blocks his pratfall into the flower cart while Richard Branson rummages and Matt Le Blanc watches.

"Sometimes, you just say, wait a minute. I'm a human being. I can go out," says Matthew Perry. "And then you realize, no, you can't. I can't tell you how many times I've just stayed home because of that fact." Here, Virgin mega-mogul Richard Branson gets a taste of what it's like to be a star on Friends as he looks over his shoulder to discover a phalanx of photographers (including ours) shooting his bull session with Matthew Perry and Matt Le Blanc.

                              CHANDLER
(THEN, TO JOEY) If you wear that hat in public, you're spending the rest of
the day alone.

JOEY PUTS ON THE HAT.
                         CHANDLER (CON'T.)
            I mean it.

JOEY COCKS THE HAT AT A RAKISH ANGLE.

                                JOEY
            Hey, if you're gonna make me choose between you and the hat — then I
            choose the hat.
                              VENDOR
            Good choice.
                            CHANDLER
            That's it. I'm outta here. I'm not going to be embarrassed anymore.

CHANDLER STARTS TO WALK AWAY, BUT IMMEDIATELY TRIPS OVER SOME OF THE
VENDOR'S PARAPHERNALIA ON THE GROUND. HE TRIES TO REGAIN HIS BALANCE, BUT IS
UNSUCCESSFUL. MUSTERING WHAT DIGNITY HE CAN, HE WALKS OFF.

                                                            CUT TO:

                            SCENE P

INT. ROSS'S HOTEL SUITE - LONDON - NIGHT (NIGHT 2) (Ross, Emily) EMILY ENTERS. ROSS IS
GETTING DRESSED. HE IS WEARING SOCKS, BOXERS AND BUTTONING A DRESS SHIRT.

                                EMILY
            (CALLING OFF) Hello.

                                ROSS
            Hey. I spoke to your dad and he seems to think we'll be able to find a new
            place for the wedding.

                                EMILY
            We don't have to. Monica and I were talking. And I was so upset about the
            hall being knocked down. And she suggested that we just put the wedding
            off for a bit.

                                ROSS
            She said what?
                                EMILY
            She said if I'm not going to be happy getting married in some place we could
            find in a day, then we should just postpone it.

ROSS STARTS TO PUT ON HIS PANTS.

                                114

ROSS

(INCREASINGLY AGITATED) Postpone it? Do you think Monica realizes what our parents spent on this wedding? Do you think my sister's teeny-tiny brain comprehends that people took time out of their lives to fly thousands of miles to be here? (RE: THE PANTS) This isn't right!

HE REALIZES HIS PANTS ARE ON BACKWARDS. HE TAKES THEM OFF.

EMILY

Look, I realize people are going to be disappointed. But I'm sure they'll come back when we can do it right.

ROSS

(GESTURING WITH PANTS) I can't ask people to do that! Would you ask people to do that?

EMILY

(ALSO GETTING UPSET) Don't you point your pants at me! We have no choice. Anywhere half-decent will have been booked months ago. Don't you understand. This is our wedding I'm talking about!

ROSS

(PUTTING ON PANTS AGAIN) All I understand is: postponing it is not an option.

EMILY

So, what are you saying? It's now or never?

ROSS

No. I'm saying it's _now_.

EMILY

Or?

ROSS

There's no "or" in mine.
(REALIZING THE PANTS ARE BACKWARDS AGAIN)
    What is wrong with these pants?!

HE RIPS THEM OFF AND PUTS THEM ON AGAIN CORRECTLY.

EMILY

You know what? It's not the pants! It's _you_ that's backwards! And if you don't understand how important this is to me, then perhaps we shouldn't be getting married at all!

SHE STORMS OUT. AS ROSS STARTS AFTER HER, HE ZIPS UP HIS PANTS.

ROSS

Emily! Emily, wait! (CATCHING HIMSELF IN THE ZIPPER) Aaggh!

ON ROSS'S PAIN, WE...   FADE OUT.

                    END OF ACT ONE

<u>ACT TWO</u>

<u>SCENE B</u>

FADE IN: <u>INT. MONICA & RACHEL'S APT. - LATER</u> (DAY 2) (Rachel, Phoebe) PHOEBE IS HANGING OUT ON THE COUCH. <u>RACHEL ENTERS</u>, CARRYING A LOT OF SHOPPING BAGS. AD-LIB HELLOS.

PHOEBE
Did shopping help you feel any better about Ross?

RACHEL
Manhattan doesn't have enough stores.

PHOEBE
(THINKS) I can help you get over Ross.

RACHEL
You can?

PHOEBE
Yeah, I just need you to bring me some photos of Ross, one small piece of chocolate and a glass of tepid water.

In this draft of the script, Rachel's self-prescribed get-over-Ross therapy has been reduced to a single shopping spree. When that doesn't work, Phoebe (literally) knocks some sense into her pretty head.

DURING THE FOLLOWING, RACHEL GRABS SOME PICTURES FROM A DRAWER, GETS THE CHOCOLATE AND A GLASS OF WATER FROM THE KITCHEN.

RACHEL
Ooh, is this one of those things where we, like, throw everything into a bag filled with graveyard dirt and hang it from a north-facing tree?

PHOEBE
(OBVIOUS) Only if you have the hiccups, too. (THEN) The only thing that's for you is the pictures. The chocolate and water are for me, because I didn't want to get up.

RACHEL BRINGS THE ITEMS OVER TO PHOEBE AND SITS NEXT TO HER.

PHOEBE (CON'T.)
Okay. Now, I'm going to hold up a picture of Ross and you are going to remember all the bad things about him. Really focus on his flaws.

RACHEL
I can do that. I certainly did it while we were going out.

PHOEBE
Before we get started, I just want to say that I love Ross. I think he's such a great guy.

PHOEBE
Okay, close your eyes. Imagine you're with Ross.

RACHEL
Okay...

PHOEBE
Now, imagine that you're with Ross and that you're kissing him. Running your hands all over his body. You run your hands through his hair, but eew! Gross! It's all covered in some kind of grease.

RACHEL
(NOSTALGIC) I don't know. I never minded his hair so much. It was always more crunchy than it was greasy.

PHOEBE
This is going to be harder than I thought. (NEW IDEA) Let's try a little aversion therapy. (HOLDING UP A PICTURE) Look at Ross.

RACHEL
Okay.

PHOEBE
Now...

SHE WHISKS THE PICTURE AWAY AND SLAPS RACHEL'S FACE.

                    RACHEL
Ow!

                    PHOEBE
How do you feel now?

                    RACHEL
Well...I like <u>you</u> less.

                                        CUT TO:

                    SCENE T

<u>INT. CHANDLER & JOEY'S HOTEL ROOM - LONDON - NIGHT</u> (NIGHT 2) (Joey, Chandler, Monica, Ross, Sarah Ferguson (On Video) CHANDLER IS THERE, BORED. <u>JOEY ENTERS</u>, STILL WEARING THE HAT. THERE IS TENSION BETWEEN THEM.

                    JOEY
Hey.

                    CHANDLER
Hey.

                    JOEY
(TAKING OFF HAT, SARCASTIC) Oh, sorry.

                    118

CHANDLER
No, no. That's okay. Look I'm sorry I said you embarrassed me. That really wasn't cool. If it makes you feel any better, I had a really lousy day.

JOEY
Me, too.

CHANDLER
Really?

JOEY
No! I had the best day ever! Check it out.

JOEY TAKES OUT THE VIDEO CAMERA AND PRESSES PLAY. THE GUYS WATCH THE MONITOR ON THE VIDEO CAMERA. MONICA ENTERS.

MONICA
Hey.

JOEY
Ssshhh.

MONICA REACTS. THE GUYS WATCH THE SCREEN. CUT TO: THE VIDEO. WE SEE BIG BEN.

JOEY (ON VIDEO O.S.)
Okay so say hi to my friend and tell him you like my hat.

WOMAN (ON VIDEO; O.S.)
What's your friend's name?

JOEY (ON VIDEO; O.S.)
Chandler.

WOMAN (ON VIDEO; O.S.)
Hi Chandler.

> It was great to meet a real live Duchess. She is really good fun.
> MATTHEW PERRY

THE WOMAN STEPS INTO FRAME AND WE SEE IT IS SARAH FERGUSON.

CHANDLER/MONICA (O.S.)
Oh, my god. That's... that's...

JOEY
Fergie, baby!

SARAH FERGUSON
Joey says you don't like his hat but I think it's really quite dashing.

JOEY STOPS THE VIDEO.

JOEY

So I was trying to figure out how to get to Buckingham Palace and I'm in my map…

ROSS ENTERS.

ROSS

(TO MONICA) So, I understand you had a little talk with Emily.

MONICA

(SMUG) I did. And you are welcome.

ROSS

Am I? And it was your idea to postpone the wedding?

MONICA

(SENSING HIS TONE, EVASIVE) Um…

CHANDLER

I'm gonna go to the bathroom.

JOEY

Wait up.

CHANDLER EXITS TO THE BATHROOM, FOLLOWED BY JOEY.

ROSS

Hey, since you're the fix-it lady, here's a pickle: what do you do when the bride says she doesn't want to have the wedding at all?

MONICA

She said that?! Why?

ROSS

I don't know. I told her it was stupid to postpone the wedding just because the hall was gone and she flipped out.

MONICA

Oh, my god. You're even dumber than I am.

ROSS

Excuse me?

MONICA

How long have you been planning this wedding?

Rumour: The Queen banned the *Friends* crew from filming a sequence in front of Buckingham Palace because she was unhappy with some unflattering remarks Fergie, who was guest-starring in the episode, had made on Oprah Winfrey's chat show.

Fact: The Palace administration only allows the Queen's London residence to be filmed for documentaries and news items. An official stressed that there could be no exceptions, even for the monarch's former daughter-in-law.

"Oh my god!" Monica gently chides Ross, "You're even dumber than I am!"

ROSS

I don't know. A month?

MONICA

Okay. Emily's probably been planning it since she was five. Ever since the first time she hung her pillowcase off the back of her head. That's what we did. We dreamed about the perfect wedding. In the perfect place. With the perfect four-tiered wedding cake – with the little people on top.

THE BATHROOM DOOR OPENS, A BOX OF TISSUES IS TOSSED OUT. ROSS CATCHES IT AND HANDS IT TO MONICA. THEN:

MONICA (CON'T.)

And the most important part is that it's with the perfect guy who understands how important all that other stuff is.

ROSS TAKES THIS IN. THEN:

ROSS

I had no idea. (THEN) That pillowcase thing? I thought you guys were just doing the "Flying Nun".

MONICA

Sometimes we were.

ROSS

(BEAT) Come on. You gotta help me figure out what to do.

Sarah Ferguson

*f*or the Duchess of York, as with Tom Conti, Jennifer Saunders and Richard Branson, the most appealing part about making a guest-star appearance on *Friends* was the exalted stature it would give her in her children's eyes. And the news did indeed have the desired effect. Andrew, Beatrice and Eugenie are fanatic *Friends* fans and the idea that their mother was actually going to act in one of the shows set the girls squealing with excitement. They immediately got started prepping her on the show, using their own *Friends* video collection to give her a crash course on each of the characters and the storylines of the last three seasons. On the morning of her debut, they got up with her at 5am to get her dressed and ready for her 8am call. They waved good-bye as her car drove away towards the Palace of Westminster and withdrew back into the house to count the minutes till it was their turn to meet the cast later that night. Fergie reports that she surprised herself by being nervous, so nervous that she was shaking. She'd done commercials and appeared on so many chat shows that she'd stopped counting them, but this was different. This time she had to act. Maybe they would even want her to be funny.

But the gallant Matt Le Blanc, her co-star in the scene, came to her rescue and worked with her on her line readings. And Matthew Perry loosened her up by making her laugh. Nervous? You'd never know it to look at the finished product. Fergie was totally cool on camera. The consensus among her co-stars: she's a natural.

> "Matt Le Blanc, with his deep, dark brown eyes, was like a knight in shining armour," says the Duchess of York, "and lulled me into a quiet confidence so I was no longer visibly shaking as I stood in front of the 30-person production team."

"Matthew Perry stayed behind to offer me further support. He's such a quick-witted actor with the ability to really test your mental agility."

"It was just like the movies," said the Duchess of York of the Friends filming. "Silence! Rolling! Action! Cut! I went along with the professionals trying not to look out of place."

"I'm ready for my close-up Mr Bright" Fergie gets gorgeous before her big scene with Matt Le Blanc

"Now, tell me again Marta, what is my motivation in this scene?"

<u>ROSS EXITS</u>. <u>MONICA FOLLOWS</u>. AFTER A MOMENT, THE BATHROOM DOOR OPENS. <u>CHANDLER AND JOEY WALK OUT</u>.

> CHANDLER
>
> Pretty intense.

> JOEY
>
> I hope Ross didn't think we were just going in there 'cause we were uncomfortable being out here.

> CHANDLER
>
> (BEAT) I hope he did.

DISSOLVE TO:

<u>SCENE W</u>

<u>INT. MONICA & RACHEL'S APT./CHANDLER & JOEY'S HOTEL ROOM - LONDON - LATER</u> (DAY 2/NIGHT 2) (Rachel, Phoebe, Joey) PHOEBE AND RACHEL ARE AS WE LEFT THEM. <u>SFX: PHONE RINGS</u>.

> PHOEBE
>
> (PICKING IT UP) Hello.

INTERCUT WITH: <u>INT. JOEY'S HOTEL ROOM - LONDON - SAME TIME</u>

> JOEY
>
> Hey, Pheebs, it's Joey.

> PHOEBE
>
> Hey, I saw a guy who looked just like you on the subway. I almost went up to him to say hi, but then I figured he doesn't care that he looks like you.

> JOEY
>
> (BEAT) That just cost me four bucks. (THEN) Listen, I just wanted to see how the chick and the duck are doing.

> PHOEBE
>
> Oh, they've been having a good time with Aunt Phoebe. (WHISPERED) Aunt Rachel hasn't been helpful at all. (THEN) So, do you miss me?

> JOEY
>
> Kinda. But I've just been having too much fun.

> PHOEBE
>
> Homesick yet?

                         JOEY
No, I don't think so.

                         PHOEBE
Well, the seven of us miss you.

                         JOEY
Who's "seven"?

                         PHOEBE
Me, Rach, the birds and the babies.

                         JOEY
(TOUCHED) Aww, the babies miss me?

SFX: KNOCK AT THE DOOR

                    PHOEBE (CON'T.)
Oh, good, there's the pizza guy.

                         JOEY
(HURT) You got pizza? Without me?

                         PHOEBE
Yup. But we were thinking about you. We ordered the Joey Special.

                         JOEY
Two pizzas?

                         PHOEBE
Yup, gotta go. Talk to you later.

                         JOEY
Wait. Where did you get it from?

BUT PHOEBE HAS HUNG UP. END INTERCUT. JOEY HANGS UP, A LITTLE BUMMED. HE TURNS
ON THE TV. SFX: "CHEERS" THEME SONG.

                    JOEY (CON'T.)
(SURPRISED) Oh.

JOEY SMILES AT FIRST. BUT AS THE SONG CONTINUES, HE SEEMS MORE MOROSE. AS HIS
LIP BEGINS TO QUIVER, WE...

                                                        CUT TO:

> *Phoebe's song about babies (before she was pregnant with three babies herself):*
>
> *"They're tiny and chubby and so sweet to touch. But soon they'll grow up. And resent you so much!!"*

SCENE X1

SCENE OMITTED

SCENE X2

INT. MONTGOMERY HALL - LONDON - MOMENTS LATER (NIGHT 2) (Ross, Monica, Emily)
MONICA AND EMILY ENTER THE DARK HALL.

                          ROSS
    Monica, why have you brought me here of all places?

                          MONICA
    You'll see.

                          EMILY
    I'm sorry, this wedding is not going to happen.

AT THAT MOMENT, THE PLACE LIGHTS UP. TWINKLY LIGHTS HAVE BEEN STRUNG FROM WALL
TO WALL. IT'S INCREDIBLY ROMANTIC. ROSS IS HOLDING THE EXTENSION CORD HE'S JUST
PLUGGED IN.

                          EMILY (CON'T.)
    Oh, my god...

                          ROSS
    Okay, but imagine a lot more lights. And fewer bricks.
    And flowers and candles.

                          MONICA
    And the musicians can go over here...and the chairs
    can face this way. (TO ROSS) You go.

                          ROSS
    But if you don't love this, we can do it any other place,
    any other time. Really. It's fine. Whatever you want.

                          EMILY
    (TEARS IN HER EYES) This is perfect.

                          ROSS
    And if it starts to rain —

                          EMILY
    We'll get wet.

HE SMILES. SHE KISSES HIM. AS THE KISS GOES ON...

> Once we had the right building façade for Montgomery Hall, we had to create three different looks for the interior sets. The first was to be strewn with bricks and debris. For the second, when Ross and Monica take Emily back to the Hall, it had to look charming enough to win her over. I translated the script's set note to mean that it should look like something out of *A Midsummer Night's Dream* – kind of magical and organic – that Monica could do herself.
> GREG GRANDE,
> SET DESIGNER

MONICA

(MOVED) Uch. And I don't even have a date.

THEY TURN TO HER AND INCLUDE HER IN THE HUG.

CUT TO:

SCENE Y

INT. MONICA & RACHEL'S APT. - THE NEXT DAY (DAY 3) (Rachel, Phoebe) PHOEBE IS GOING THROUGH MORE PICTURES. SHE STOPS AT ONE AND CALLS OFF TO RACHEL:

RACHEL

Pheebs, do you remember where the duck food is?

PHOEBE

Yeah, in the guys' apartment under the sink. Why?

RACHEL, WEARING AN OVERCOAT, ENTERS FROM HER BEDROOM, CARRYING A SUITCASE.

RACHEL

I'm going to London.

PHOEBE

What? What do you mean you're going to London?

RACHEL

I have to tell Ross I love him. Now you take care and don't have those babies till I get back.

PHOEBE

But you can't go. Ross loves Emily.

RACHEL

I know he does. I have to tell him how I feel. I just think he should have all the information and then he can make an informed decision.

PHOEBE

That's not why you're going. You're going there because you hope he's going to say, "Oh, I love you, too, Rach. Forget about that British chippy."

RACHEL

(HOPEFUL) You think he will?

127

PHOEBE
No! Because he's in love with the British chippy. Rachel, if you go you're just going to mess with his head and ruin his wedding. Rachel, it's too late. You missed your chance. I'm sorry. I know this must be really hard, but it's over.

THIS HITS RACHEL. SHE SITS. RELIEVED, PHOEBE SITS AS WELL. THEN:

RACHEL
(DETERMINED) It's not over till someone says "I do."

WITH THAT, SHE STANDS UP, GRABS HER BAG, AND HEADS FOR THE DOOR.

PHOEBE
(DESPERATE) Okay, I do! I do! I do!

RACHEL EXITS..

PHOEBE (CON'T.)
It's not like I can really chase you. I'm carrying a litter.

FADE OUT.

END OF ACT TWO

- ACT THREE –

SCENE Z

FADE IN: INT. WALTHAM'S RESIDENCE - LONDON/MONICA & RACHEL'S APT. - NIGHT/DAY
(NIGHT 3/DAY 3) (Phoebe, Housekeeper) WE SEE A WALL OF EMILY'S PARENTS' HOUSE. THERE
IS A TELEPHONE. IT RINGS. A HOUSEKEEPER ENTERS AND ANSWERS.

HOUSEKEEPER

Waltham residence.

INTERCUT WITH: INT. MONICA & RACHEL'S APT. - SAME TIME

PHOEBE

Yes. Is this Emily's parents' house?

HOUSEKEEPER

Yes, this is the housekeeper. And by the way, young lady, that is not how one
addresses a person on the telephone. First one identifies oneself, and then
politely asks for the party with whom one wishes to speak.

PHOEBE

This is Phoebe Buffay. I was wondering, please, if it's not too much trouble,
please, if I might speak with Emily Waltham, please.

HOUSEKEEPER

Miss Waltham's at the rehearsal dinner. And it's not polite to make fun of
people. Goodbye.

PHOEBE

No, wait. I'll be nice. I just need the number for where they are.

HOUSEKEEPER

I'm sorry. I'm not at liberty to give that out.

PHOEBE

Listen somebody's on their way to ruin the wedding And I need to warn
somebody. So, if you don't give me that number, I'm going to come over
there and kick your snooty ass all the way to …New Glouken…shire! (THEN)
Hello? Hello? (THEN) She knew I could kick her ass.

CUT TO:

JUDY

Sorry we're late. I insisted on riding the tube.

JACK

Judy please! The kids…

JUDY

Jack, that's what they call the subway.

JACK

Oh. I thought…

ROSS

Dad, dad – that's okay.

EMILY

Here's my dad and stepmom. Mr. and Mrs. Geller, this is Steven and Andrea Waltham.

> "There was this tabloid in England that takes the heads of celebrities and puts them on shots of naked women – which is libellous, of course, but somehow they get away with it. Anyway, they did it with Courteney and Jennifer while we were in London shooting, so we – the guys and I – hid it from them."
>
> ELLIOTT GOULD

STEVEN WALTHAM

Andrea, darling, it's the Gellers. (ON HER MOBILE PHONE: NO RESPONSE) It's the Gellers, darling. (TO THE GELLERS) I'm sorry, she's horribly self-involved, I don't know why I married her.

ANDREA WALTHAM

(GETTING OFF THE PHONE) Sorry, what?

STEVEN WALTHAM

It's the Gellers, darling.

ANDREA WALTHAM

Where?

STEVEN WALTHAM

(INDICATING THE GELLERS) Well, that's one. And that's another one.

AD-LIB GREETINGS.

STEVEN WALTHAM (CONT.)

Terribly nice of you to offer to pay for half the wedding.

JACK GELLER

Forget about it. The hell with tradition. We're happy to do it.

JUDY GELLER

We know how expensive weddings are. Besides, it may be the only wedding we get to throw.

MONICA

(PAINED LAUGH) A joke that's funny in all countries.

MEANWHILE, ACROSS THE ROOM, A WAITER IS OFFERING JOEY AND CHANDLER A TRAY OF HORS D'OUEVRES.

JOEY

What's in it?

WAITER

Goat cheese, watercress and pancetta.

JOEY

(TO CHANDLER, UPSET) That's not food. Everything's different here. I want to go home. I miss my family. I miss the coffee house. I can't even remember what Phoebe looks like.

CHANDLER

You've been here for <u>three days</u>! How can you be homesick? Now, will you please relax and try to enjoy yourself?

JOEY STARES AT CHANDLER FOR A BEAT. THEN...

JOEY

(UPSET) You're different here, too. You're mean in England.

> "I let it be known that I wanted to do something on *Friends* the minute I found out that it was coming to London. I wasn't shy about it, I can tell you. But then, I'm a great fan of the show. I've seen all the shows and read all the books. And my kids, well, they're absolutely wild about it. They're the biggest reason I wanted to do the show."
>
> JENNIFER SAUNDERS

MEANWHILE, ACROSS THE ROOM, JACK SITS AT A TABLE STUDYING HIS HALF OF THE BILL. IT'S SEVERAL PAGES LONG. ROSS, MONICA AND JUDY ARE TALKING NEARBY.

JACK GELLER

What the hell... ?

MONICA/ROSS

What's the matter, Dad? What's up?

JACK GELLER

This bill for my half of the wedding. It's insane.

JUDY GELLER

How can it be so much? The reception's at their house.

JACK GELLER

(READING) Flowers... Liquor... Re-carpet first floor? New guest bath? Landscaping!? I'm paying to remodel this guy's house! (THEN) I'm gonna give that son-of-a-bitch a piece of my mind.

ROSS

Dad, please. I don't want anything to upset Emily tonight. She's had a hard enough couple of days as it is. Let me go talk to him, okay?

ROSS TAKES THE BILL AND STARTS OFF. JACK CALLS AFTER:

JACK GELLER

You tell him no one takes advantage of the Gellers!

JUDY GELLER

(KIND OF TURNED ON) Oh, Jack. Sometimes I forget how powerful you can be.

MONICA

(ICKED OUT) And I'm gonna go get drunk.

CUT TO:

SCENE BB

INT. AIRPORT TICKET COUNTER - AFTERNOON (DAY 3)

TICKET AGENT

(EXTREMELY CHEERFULLY) Hello!

RACHEL

(EQUALLY CHEERFULLY) Hello! (THEN, FRANTIC) When is your next flight to London?

TICKET AGENT

There's one leaving in thirty minutes... (CHECKING COMPUTER) And I do have one seat left.

RACHEL

Thank you. Thank you. Thank you.

TICKET AGENT

The last-minute fare on this ticket is twenty-seven hundred dollars.

RACHEL

It's just I don't have that much left on my credit card.

TICKET AGENT

You can split it with another credit card.

RACHEL

How 'bout five cards?

TICKET AGENT

I'm just going to need to see your passport.

> The people I've met here in England are absolutely lovely and kind and funny. And there's this air about the place. I don't know what it is – it's very British!.
> JENNIFER ANISTON

RACHEL REACTS. OBVIOUSLY, SHE'S FORGOTTEN HER PASSPORT. RACHEL THINKS A BEAT, THEN...

RACHEL
Okay, I don't have it with me,
but I <u>can</u> tell you exactly where
it is on my night stand.

RACHEL (CON'T.)
(OFF HER LOOK) I have my
driver's license... and (WITH A
WINK) a twenty?

ON THE TICKET AGENT'S IMPASSIVE
STARE, WE...

CUT TO:

<u>SCENE CC</u>
<u>SCENE OMITTED</u>

<u>SCENE CCX</u>

<u>INT. RESTAURANT - LONDON - A LITTLE LATER</u> (NIGHT 3) ROSS AND THE WALTHAMS ARE
DEEP IN NEGOTIATIONS. MR. WALTHAM IS SMOKING A CIGARETTE. ROSS NURSES A
SCOTCH.

ROSS
I'm sorry, my father is not paying for your built-in bar-b-que. And believe me,
you can kiss your gazebo goodbye. I might be able to get you the new lawn.

STEVEN WALTHAM
Then you've got to give me the lawn ornaments.

ROSS
I go back there with lawn ornaments, he's going to laugh in my face.

ANDREA WALTHAM
This is ridiculous. We had an agreement. Steven, say something!

STEVEN WALTHAM
Don't take that tone with me.

SHE GIVES HIM A SCARY LOOK.

STEVEN WALTHAM
All right, you can.

AS ROSS RUBS HIS TEMPLES, WE...

CUT TO:

SCENE DD

INT. MONICA & RACHEL'S APT. - A BIT LATER (DAY 3)
PHOEBE IS IN A CHAIR. RACHEL BURSTS IN.

> RACHEL
>
> (OUT OF BREATH) Hi, Pheebs.

> PHOEBE
>
> O, thank god, you changed your mind.

RACHEL SPRINTS INTO HER ROOM. PHOEBE CALLS AFTER:

> PHOEBE (CON'T.)
>
> I understand if you're not ready to talk. But I want you to know I think you're doing the right thing. And —

RACHEL EMERGES FROM HER BEDROOM, HOLDING HER PASSPORT. SHE HEADS FOR THE DOOR.

> RACHEL
>
> Bye, Pheebs.

> PHOEBE
>
> Wait, where are you going?

RACHEL EXITS. PHOEBE STRUGGLES TO GET UP, BUT FAILS.

> PHOEBE
>
> Wait! Wait! Wait! Uch, why am I always pregnant when she does that?!

CUT TO:

SCENE HH

INT. RESTAURANT - LONDON/MONICA & RACHEL'S APT. - A LITTLE LATER (NIGHT 3/DAY 3)
(Ross, Chandler, Monica, Joey, Phoebe, Emily, Steven Waltham, Andrea Waltham, Jack Geller, Judy Geller, Felicity, Extras) EVERYONE HAS FINISHED EATING. CHANDLER STANDS UP AND CLINKS HIS GLASS. EVERYONE QUIETS DOWN.

> CHANDLER
>
> Thank you. I'd like to propose a toast to Ross and Emily. Now, of course, my big toast is tomorrow night after the wedding. So this is just my little toast — or Melba toast, if you will...

CHANDLER WAITS FOR THE BIG LAUGH. IT DOESN'T COME.

CHANDLER (CON'T.)
Okay. I've known Ross for a long time. In fact, I knew him when he was dating his first girlfriend. It looked like things were really going to work out, until one day he <u>over-inflated</u> her. (NO RESPONSE) Oh, dear god...

MEANWHILE, MRS. WALTHAM'S MOBILE PHONE RINGS. SHE TAKES IT OUT OF HER PURSE.

ANDREA WALTHAM
Hello? Waltham Interiors.

INTERCUT WITH: <u>INT. MONICA & RACHEL'S APT. - SAME TIME</u>

Phoebe has got a lot of ass to kick – as soon as she's not carrying a litter.

PHOEBE

Mrs. Waltham, hi. I need to talk to either one of the best men, or Ross's sister, Monica.

ANDREA WALTHAM

Who is this?

PHOEBE

This is Phoebe Buffay. I'm one of Ross's best friends.

ANDREA WALTHAM

If you're one of Ross's best friends, why aren't you here?

PHOEBE

I can't fly because I'm having my brother's babies.

ANDREA WALTHAM

Am I on the radio?

PHOEBE

No. Can I talk to one of them? It's very important.

ANDREA WALTHAM

No, I'm bored with you now. I'm going to cut you off.

WITH THAT, MRS. WALTHAM HANGS UP.

PHOEBE

Okay, I'm going to have to kick her ass too.

> "The writers were very good with letting us do our own, well, interpretation of Andrea and Steven. We did some improvisation at the rehearsals and then they wrote what we'd done into the script. We managed to make the Walthams even more despicable than the writers had originally written them."
> JENNIFER SAUNDERS

CHANDLER

...And I'm sure we're all very excited to see Ross and Emily get married tomorrow over at Montgomery Hall. To think, my friend married in Monty Hall?! (AGAIN, NOTHING) Come on, Monty Hall?! "Let's Make a Deal"?!

STEVEN WALTHAM LOOKS TO HIS WIFE, PUZZLED. SHE SHRUGS.

CHANDLER (CON'T.)

(DISGUSTED) Ah, forget it. Congratulations Ross and Emily.

HE SITS. JOEY STANDS.

JOEY

Hey. Best man number two, Joey Tribbiani. Okay, I'm not good with the jokes, like Chandler. I just wanted to say congratulations to the happy couple. I first met Ross in this coffee house back home... (GETTING A LITTLE MISTY) Home... New York City... where everybody knows my name. (THEN) Anyway, I love you guys. But not as much as I love America! (SITTING, TO CHANDLER) Please, can we go home now?

AN UNBELIEVABLY HOT BRIDESMAID, FELICITY, COMES UP.

FELICITY
You're going home? I was hoping I'd get to know you better.

JOEY
(BEAT, BRIGHTLY) I'm not going anywhere, sweetheart.

ON JOEY'S HAPPY SMILE, WE...   CUT TO:

SCENE JJ

INT. RESTAURANT - LONDON - A LITTLE LATER (NIGHT 3) THE REHEARSAL DINNER IS
WRAPPING UP. PEOPLE ARE STARTING TO LEAVE. MONICA IS COMFORTING CHANDLER.

MONICA
I was laughing.

CHANDLER
Out loud?

MONICA
Well, I didn't want people to think I was stupid.

HE REACTS. SHE HUGS HIM. HE SMILES AT HER.

CHANDLER
So, how are you doing?

MONICA
I'm okay. My mom's driving me crazy. But you know, Ross is getting married
and I'm happy. I'm not going to let anything spoil that.

AN OLDER, INTOXICATED GUEST COMES OVER.

OLDER GUEST
(TO MONICA) I just want to say that Ross is a wonderful young man.

MONICA
(WITH A SMILE) We like him.

OLDER GUEST
My god, you must have been a teenager when you had him.

MONICA'S JAW DROPS AND CHANDLER'S EYES GO WIDE. MEANWHILE, ROSS IS TRYING TO
REASON WITH THE PARENTS.

JACK GELLER
(ADAMANT) There's no way in hell I'm paying for it.

"All right! That's it! Parents, back away! This is our wedding day! From now on, everyone gets along! And if I hear one more word: no grandchildren!"

ROSS
Look, we're down to just one point. Could we maybe please settle this after the wedding?

JACK GELLER
(REASONABLE) All right, fine. But I just want to say (TO MR. WALTHAM) I'm not paying for your wine cellar, you thieving, would-be-speaking-German-if-it-weren't-for-us, cheap little man!

THE GELLERS EXIT.

MEANWHILE, CHANDLER IS STILL WITH MONICA.

CHANDLER
The guy was hammered. There is no way you look like Ross's mother.

MONICA
Then why would he say it?!

CHANDLER

Because he's crazy! He came up to me earlier and thanked me for my very moving performance in *Titanic*.

MONICA

(UPSET) My mom's right. I'm never going to get married.

CHANDLER

That's ridiculous. Who wouldn't want you?

MONICA

Oh, please. I'm a single mom with a thirty year old son!

AS CHANDLER COMFORTS HER, WE...

DISSOLVE TO:

SCENE KK

INT. AIRPORT TICKET COUNTER - LATER (NIGHT 3) RACHEL IS ABLE TO RUN RIGHT UP TO THE TICKET COUNTER.

RACHEL

Hi, I'm back. Listen, I need to –

TICKET AGENT

(EXTREMELY CHEERFUL) Hello!

RACHEL

Right, hello. I need to get on the eleven o'clock flight to London.

TICKET AGENT

I'm sorry. That plane has already pulled away from the gate.

RACHEL

Okay, you're just gonna have to call the plane back to pick me up.

TICKET AGENT

RACHEL

(CONSPIRATORIALLY) Come on, we can just tell them there's a problem with the (AIR QUOTES) "engine".

TICKET AGENT

I'm going to have to ask you to step aside, miss.

RACHEL

Look, if I don't get to London, he's going to marry this other girl!

TICKET AGENT

I can't imagine why.

RACHEL

All right. I am not leaving here until you call that plane back.

THE TICKET AGENT FLIPS UP THE "CLOSED" SIGN, TAKES THREE STEPS TO THE NEXT COUNTER.

CUT TO:

SCENE MM

INT. CHANDLER & JOEY'S HOTEL ROOM - LONDON - NEXT MORNING (DAY 4) ROSS BURSTS IN. CHANDLER IS IN BED, ASLEEP.

ROSS

(BEAMING) I'm getting married today!

CHANDLER

(WAKING UP) What? Huh?

ROSS

I'm getting married!

CHANDLER

(THUMBS UP) Whoohoo!

ROSS EXITS. MONICA POKES HER HEAD OUT FROM UNDER THE COVERS.

MONICA

(FREAKED) Do you think he knew I was here?

FADE OUT.

END OF ACT THREE

They got together in London ... But will they stay together in New York?

"When we did decide to go ahead and get Chandler and Monica together we knew we wanted to totally surprise the audience, to spring it on them out of the blue. We also had to work in a lot of stuff that would help the audience understand what it would take to get Monica there: like her mother driving her crazy, the drunk guy thinking she was Ross's mother, and her getting drunk herself."

MICHAEL BORKOW

Courteney Cox and Matthew Perry kick back during a rehearsal break.

– <u>ACT FOUR</u> –

<u>SCENE PP</u>

FADE IN: <u>INT. CHANDLER & JOEY'S HOTEL ROOM - LONDON - CONTINUOUS</u> (DAY 4)
CHANDLER AND MONICA ARE BOTH TOTALLY FREAKED OUT. THEY CAN'T LOOK AT
EACH OTHER.

> CHANDLER
> So. I've never done that with you before.

> MONICA
> Nooo.

> CHANDLER
> So, how you doing?

> MONICA
> Yup. You?

> CHANDLER
> Yeah. Fine. You? (OFF HER LOOK) We did you.

> MONICA
> I better get going —

> CHANDLER
> Absolutely.

SHE STARTS TO GET OUT OF BED. THEN STOPS.

> MONICA
> Could you not look?

> CHANDLER
> I don't wanna look.

HE LOOKS AWAY. SHE STARTS TO GET OUT OF BED.

CUT TO:

> "The truth of the matter
> is, kissing a pretty actress
> is not a romantic or sexy
> situation. It's all angles,
> lights ... It's all technical,
> move your shoulder here.
> There are fifty people
> watching, boom
> operators, script
> supervisors. It's not a
> sexy thing."
> MATTHEW PERRY

142

He's got her number. Hugh Laurie as "The Gentleman" sums up the entire Ross–Rachel contretemps in a nutshell.

<u>SCENE PPX</u>
<u>INT. AIRPLANE - LATER</u> (DAY 4)

RACHEL IS IN HER SEAT, WAITING TO TAKE OFF. SHE ANXIOUSLY TAPS AND DRUMS.

GENTLEMAN
If you're planning on doing that for the entire flight, please tell me now, so I can take a sedative. Or perhaps slip you one.

RACHEL
(STOPPING) I'm sorry. I'm sorry. (BEAT, THEN) It's just, I'm kinda excited. I'm going to London to tell this guy I love him.

HE LOOKS AT HER FOR A BEAT, THEN TURNS AWAY AND PUTS ON HIS HEADPHONES.

CUT TO:

<u>SCENE RR</u>

<u>INT. CHANDLER & JOEY'S HOTEL ROOM - LONDON/MONICA & RACHEL'S APT. - SAME TIME</u> (DAY 4) <u>JOEY ENTERS</u>. HE PICKS UP THE PHONE.

JOEY
Hello?

INTERCUT WITH: <u>INT. MONICA & RACHEL'S APT. - SAME TIME</u>. PHOEBE IS ON THE PHONE.

PHOEBE

Where the hell have you been?!

JOEY

Hey. I spent the night out. I met this cute bridesmaid. Oh, man, she is so –

PHOEBE

I don't want to hear about her!

JOEY

Aw, Pheebs. You know you're still my number one girl.

PHOEBE

No! We have an emergency! Rachel is coming to London!

JOEY

Oh, great!

PHOEBE

No, not great! She's coming to tell Ross she loves him.

JOEY

But he loves Emily.

PHOEBE

I know that. Stop her. She's going to ruin the wedding.

JOEY

Okay.

PHOEBE

So —

JOEY

Hold on. (WRITING ON PAD) "Rachel coming. Do... something."

PHOEBE

(INTENSE) So, okay. I've done my part. It's your responsibility now. The burden is off me. Right?

JOEY

Right.

PHOEBE

All right. (THEN, CHATTY) So, tell me about this girl.

CUT TO:

SCENE WW

INT. CHANDLER & JOEY'S HOTEL ROOM - LONDON - A LITTLE LATER (DAY 4)
CHANDLER EMERGES FROM THE BATHROOM IN A BATHROBE.

JOEY (CON'T.)

Have you seen Monica?

CHANDLER

(PANIC) I'm not seeing Monica.

JOEY

What?

CHANDLER

What?

"But what I really want to do is direct." Matthew Perry hijacks the set from Kevin Bright.

> JOEY

We've got to find her. Phoebe just called. Rachel's coming to tell Ross she loves him

> CHANDLER

Oh, my god.

> JOEY

I know. So, we've got to find Monica. Do you know where she is?

> CHANDLER

No! What's with the third degree?! Why don't you just shine a light in my eyes?!

ON JOEY'S BEFUDDLEMENT, WE...

CUT TO:

<u>SCENE XX</u>

<u>INT. AIRPLANE - LATER</u> (DAY 4) RACHEL IS STILL TALKING TO THE OTHER PASSENGER, DEEP INTO HER STORY.

> RACHEL

And I realized all this stuff I've been doing — proposing to Joshua, lying to Ross about why I couldn't go — it's all just a way of –

THE GENTLEMAN TAKES OFF HIS HEADPHONES.

> GENTLEMAN

If I may interrupt. I'd just like to say that you are a horrible, horrible person.

> RACHEL

Pardon me?

> GENTLEMAN

You say you love this man, and yet you're about to ruin the happiest day of his life. I'm afraid I have to agree with your friend, Pheebs, this is a terrible, terrible plan.

> RACHEL

But he's got to know how I feel.

> GENTLEMAN

Why? He loves this Emily. No good can come of this.

> RACHEL

Well, I think you're wrong.

> GENTLEMAN

(MOCK DESPAIR) Oh, no. And by the way, it seems quite clear to me that you <u>were</u> on a break.

RACHEL REACTS. THE GENTLEMAN PUTS HIS HEADPHONES BACK ON AND RETURNS TO IGNORING HER.

DISSOLVE TO:

SCENE YY

INT. MONTGOMERY HALL/ANTEROOM - LONDON - THAT NIGHT. (NIGHT 4) THE HALL HAS BEEN FULLY TRANSFORMED. IN ADDITION TO THE TWINKLY LIGHTS, FLOWERS AND CANDLES ABOUND. IT'S ABOUT AN HOUR BEFORE THE WEDDING. MONICA, ANDREA, AND JUDY ARE MARVELLING AT THE ROOM.

JUDY GELLER

It's like a fairyland...

ANDREA WALTHAM

I know, it's horrible, isn't it?

MONICA

Well, I love it. I only hope my wedding looks this good.

JUDY GELLER

I just hope —

MONICA

You can let some of them go by!

JOEY COMES OVER.

JOEY

Psst. Monica. We should really start watching out for Rachel. I'll cover the front door, and you watch that big hole at the back of the building, and I've got Chandler covering Ross.

MONICA

Why would I care where Chandler is. You know, sometimes I don't even like Chandler.

JOEY

(CONFUSED) Okay.

THEY MOVE OFF IN DIFFERENT DIRECTIONS. MEANWHILE, CHANDLER IS WITH ROSS.

ROSS

(TRYING VARIOUS READINGS) I do. I do. I do.

CHANDLER

Yeah, you're right. It's the second one.

RESET TO: INT. ANTEROOM - CONTINUOUS. JOEY'S GUARDING THE DOOR. FELICITY ENTERS.

An Interview With Greg Grande – Set Decorator

Designing A Dream Wedding

i went over to London two weeks early to scout for a partly demolished building with character that could act as the exterior of the hall where Emily and Ross were to be married. Once we had the right building, we had to create two different looks for the Hall's interior that would match the façade. The first was to look desolate – a half-demolished shell strewn with bricks and debris. The second had to look charming enough to convince Emily that there really could be a wedding there. I translated the script's set note to mean that it should look like something out of *A Midsummer Night's Dream* – kind of magical and organic. I also knew that it needed to be informal enough that Monica could have done most of it herself, while at the same time so beautiful it would make the audience gasp the first time they saw it – which I'm happy to say they did.

In addition to the wedding hall, we also had to create a banquet room for the rehearsal dinner, and Joey and Chandler's hotel room – which would also double as Ross and Emily's bridal suite. Each of these sets had to be created while we were filming – with a studio audience watching. We shot three shows in

two days, so that meant that we had to do three set conversions, three different times in two days. So, while the actors were doing a scene in the hotel room, my crew and I were recreating the next look for the restaurant or the hotel or Montgomery Hall. We were in constant motion because there was never a second when the sets didn't have to be

"I am careful to co-ordinate with Debra McGuire and the wardrobe department about colours and such. I don't want to upstage or clash with the look of the actors," says set designer Greg Grande. Here Debra McGuire upstages Greg at a Friends party following filming.

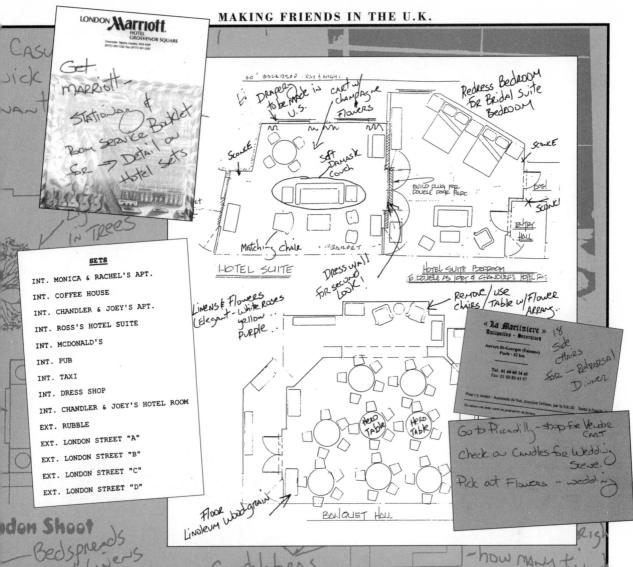

Marriott note (handwritten):
LONDON Marriott HOTEL GROSVENOR SQUARE

Get marriott stationary & room service booklet for → Detail on Hotel sets

Floor plan annotations (handwritten):
30' backdrop - Day & night
Drapery to be made in U.S.
Cart w/ champagne & flowers
Redress Bedroom for Bridal Suite Bedroom
Sconce
Soft Damask Couch
Build plug for double door here
Bath
Sconce
Entry Hall
Matching chair
Carpet
HOTEL SUITE
Dress up for second look!
HOTEL SUITE BEDROOM to double as Joey & Chandlers hotel Rm.
Remove / use chairs / table w/ flower arrang.
Linens & Flowers (Elegant - white roses yellow ... purple ..
Floor Linoleum woodgrain
BANQUET HALL
Head Table
Head Table

La Martiniere card (handwritten):
« La Martiniere » Antiquites - Decoration
Auvers-St-Georges (Essonne) Paris : 42 km
Tel. 01 60 80 34 45 Fax. 01 60 80 41 57
18 side chairs for → Rehearsal Dinner

Card (handwritten):
Go to Picadilly - stop for Veuube cart
Check on Candles for Wedding scene.
Pick out Flowers - wedding

SETS list:

- INT. MONICA & RACHEL'S APT.
- INT. COFFEE HOUSE
- INT. CHANDLER & JOEY'S APT.
- INT. ROSS'S HOTEL SUITE
- INT. MCDONALD'S
- INT. PUB
- INT. TAXI
- INT. DRESS SHOP
- INT. CHANDLER & JOEY'S HOTEL ROOM
- EXT. RUBBLE
- EXT. LONDON STREET "A"
- EXT. LONDON STREET "B"
- EXT. LONDON STREET "C"
- EXT. LONDON STREET "D"

London Shoot

Bedspreads & Linens

redressed. The rehearsal dinner, for example, had three different types of food service – hors d'oeuvres, dinner and dessert – which had to be arranged in a way that would look convincing. And levels of wine had to be lower for each progressive sequence. Of course, viewers don't really notice these details, but they're all a part of the overall feeling that makes a scene look believable.

Fortunately, I had some of the best set dressing and prop guys in the business on my London crews. Most of them had just come from working with Stanley Kubrick on *Eyes Wide Shut* and my primary liaison was Peter Young who won an Academy Award for the first *Batman*. He took me to flea markets and little boutiques and fabric shops, and places with great fabrics and carpets. I also went to Paris for the weekend – to the flea market – where I got some candelabras for the wedding that I carried back with me on the airplane.

I had a great time shopping in London and Paris, but for me, this episode was probably the hardest thing I've ever done – and that includes both television and movies. I had some good dinners out, but my time in London was mostly spent working. Things got even wilder with the arrival of the cast and crew. Organized chaos is the best way to describe that week.

Some people have asked why we went to London to shoot this episode when we could easily have recreated everything we needed in Los Angeles. The answer is: we did it for the British fans, and that made it totally wonderful and worth it. What more could you ask for than to be in London in the middle of *Friends*-mania. There were news crews and paparazzi everywhere. You would have to be crazy not to have been excited by it."

"Generally speaking, the only things Kevin, Marta, David and I really have to confer on are special pieces like Joey's hat and the walk-in map - 'hero' props that are a part of the story and have to be real and funny at the same time. The note on Joey's hat was that it had to be huge and like a top-hat in shape and have a Union Jack. The first things we found were some floppy berets, but they weren't silly enough. Then one morning I was out shopping and I saw a young French tourist walk by wearing this hysterical hat. He told me where he'd gotten it and I went there immediately. Many hours later, I put on the hat and poked my head into a late night writers' session with it and they said, 'That's it. That's the hat.'"

GREG GRANDE

☐ Friends London Shoot
Set Dressing
shop fabric
check out prop houses:
- Studio & T.V. Hire
- Set Pieces
- Eccentric Trading
- Old Times for chandaliers & candelabras
- Superhire for Joey & Chandlers Hotel Furniture
- Newman's Hire for upscale chairs artwork, Sconces etc. for Reheasal Sc.
- Lewis & Kay for Linens & such
- Camden Hire for lighting

Friends costume designer Debra McGuire saw Emily Waltham as someone who would choose a wedding gown that was simple and elegant. But it also had to be so beautiful that it would practically strike Ross speechless when he saw her in it for the first time. And it had to be so irresistible that Monica would secretly try it on when no one was around. There was also a bit of a technical problem to overcome with this particular design in that it had to disguise the fact that actress Helen Baxendale was pregnant at the time the episode was filmed – and if Emily looked like she was expecting at her wedding, it would add a whole new angle to the already hysterical proceedings.

Deb—
will her boobs look too big considering Helen's pregnant? Besides that, it's beautiful + simple

Marta:
Some ideas for the Emily "Wedding" dress. Let me know what you think?
xoxo D

Braided △'s

Braiding

Jacket? Maybe yea maybe no—
* add Bolero jacket w/braided borders

flared sleeve w/4" slit (see pattern notes!)

* leave plenty of room allow.

Debra McGuire

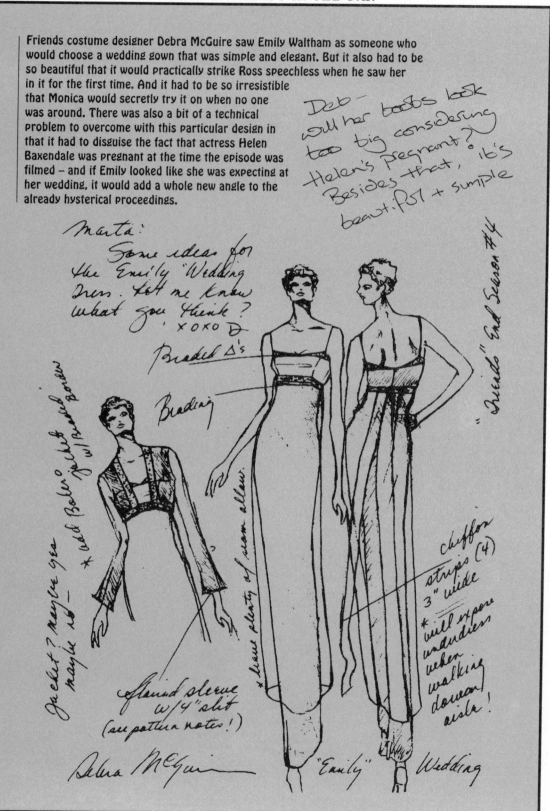

"Friends" End Season #4

chiffon strips (4) 3" wide
* will expose undundies when walking down aisle!

"Emily"   Wedding

FELICITY

Hi, Joey.

JOEY

Hey, Felicity.

FELICITY

I thought about you all day.

JOEY

Yeah?

FELICITY

(INTIMATE) Talk New York to me again.

JOEY

Fuggetaboutit.

FELICITY

Ooo...

JOEY

How you doin'?

SHE SQUEALS AND KISSES HIM. THEY DUCK BEHIND A PILLAR.

RESET TO: <u>INT. MONTGOMERY HALL - CONTINUOUS</u>. THE GELLERS AND THE WALTHAMS ARE STILL FIGHTING OVER THE BILL.

JUDY GELLER

There is nothing to discuss. We are not paying for your wine cellar!

<u>ROSS COMES OVER</u>.

STEVEN WALTHAM
(TO JACK) Look, you've got to meet me in the middle here.

JACK GELLER

Hey, you keep pushing me on this, my foot's gonna meet the middle of your ass.

<u>EMILY RUNS OUT</u>.

EMILY

What's going on?

ROSS

Don't worry, I've got everything under control.

STEVEN WALTHAM
You want a piece of me, sir? Is that it?!

ROSS

All right! That's it! Parents, back away! This is our wedding day! From now on, everyone gets along! And if I hear one more word: no grandchildren!

PARENTS

(COWED) Absolutely. You're right. Very sorry.

STEVEN WALTHAM

(TO JACK, AS THEY MOVE OFF) I could kill you with my thumb.

THE PARENTS EXIT.

EMILY

What was that about?

ROSS

Okay, there was a little disagreement over – God, you look beautiful.

EMILY

(PLEASED) Oh. (THEN) But you're not meant to see me before the wedding. It's bad luck.

ROSS

I think we've had all the bad luck we're going to have.

RESET TO: INT. ANTEROOM - CONTINUOUS. JOEY IS STILL MAKING OUT WITH FELICITY. THEY ARE UNAWARE AS RACHEL ENTERS. SHE RUSHES PAST THEM.

RESET TO: INT. MONTGOMERY HALL - CONTINUOUS. RACHEL ENTERS. SHE SEES ROSS AND EMILY. THEY ARE VERY CLOSE AND HE IS HOLDING HER HANDS. THEY KISS. RACHEL TAKES THIS IN. AFTER A MOMENT EMILY MUTTERS SOMETHING TENDER TO ROSS AND EXITS. ROSS TURNS AND SEES RACHEL.

ROSS

Oh, my god. Rachel? You're here. I can't believe it! (THEN, CURIOUS) What happened? Why are you here?

RACHEL TAKES A BEAT.

RACHEL

I came to... I just needed to tell you...congratulations.

HE SMILES AND HUGS HER.

DISSOLVE TO:

> I'm not saying that Rachel and Ross as a married couple can't be done. The problem is that if they ever do get married, the tension is gone. We saw that when they were happy, they weren't as funny. Once we broke them up, there was all sorts of great stuff to mine.
>
> MICHAEL BORKOW

153

You thought things were crazy before? You ain't seen nothin' yet.

SCENE ZZ

<u>INT. MONTGOMERY HALL - LONDON/MONICA & RACHEL'S APT. - NIGHT/DAY</u> (NIGHT 4/DAY 4) (Monica, Phoebe, Rachel, Ross, Chandler, Joey, Emily, Andrea Waltham, Steven Waltham, Jack Geller, Judy Geller, Registrar, Felicity, Musicians, Extras) THE CEREMONY IS BEGINNING. MUSIC IS PLAYING. THE LAST FEW PEOPLE FIND THEIR SEATS. ROSS STANDS AT THE FRONT. THE PROCESSIONAL HAS BEGUN. <u>JOEY ENTERS</u> FROM THE BACK <u>WITH ANDREA WALTHAM,</u> AND STARTS WALKING DOWN THE AISLE. MRS. WALTHAM'S MOBILE PHONE RINGS. SHE ANSWERS IT.

> ANDREA WALTHAM
>
> Hello? Waltham Interiors.

INTERCUT WITH: <u>INT. MONICA & RACHEL'S APT. - CONTINUOUS</u>

> PHOEBE
>
> Hi, it's Phoebe again.

> ANDREA WALTHAM
>
> (BEAT) Why?